ORGANIC UNITY IN COLERIDGE

BY

GORDON McKENZIE

FOLCROFT LIBRARY EDITIONS / 1973

Library of Congress Cataloging in Publication Data

McKenzie, Gordon, 1901–
   Organic unity in Coleridge.

   Original ed. issued as v. 7, no. 1 of University
of California publications in English.
   1. Coleridge, Samuel Taylor, 1772–1834.
I. Title. II. Series: California. University.
University of California publications in English,
v. 7, no. 1.
PR4484.M25 1973   821'.7   73–5879
ISBN 0–8414–5928–2 (lib. bdg.)

Manufactured in the United States of America.

ORGANIC UNITY IN COLERIDGE

BY

GORDON McKENZIE

University of California Publications in English
Editors: B. P. Kurtz, J. R. Caldwell, Willard Farnham
Volume 7, No. 1, pp. 1–108
Transmitted May 19, 1937
Issued March 2, 1939
Price, $1.00

University of California Press
Berkeley, California

———

Cambridge University Press
London, England

PRINTED IN THE UNITED STATES OF AMERICA

TO

BENJAMIN P. KURTZ AND

STEPHEN C. PEPPER

WITH GRATITUDE AND

AFFECTION

CONTENTS

I. INTRODUCTION

THE MOST IMPORTANT value of Coleridge for modern literary criticism lies in his attempts to formulate a method and a technique by which literature may be approached. Lesser values have in the past been more obvious. His brilliant intuitions, mistakenly called "isolated," his psychological insights, even when considered without relation to each other, help to illuminate the particular experience. But such special illuminations are relatively frequent in the history of criticism. There have been many essayists who have produced fertile hints and suggestions, splendid in themselves perhaps, but separate and structureless. Historically, there has been a lack of formulation of critical methods which are consistent, applicable, and richly productive. Coleridge felt very keenly the need for a systematic criticism and made attempts to formulate his ideas more successfully than is generally recognized. The purpose of the following pages is to demonstrate the nature of his method and technique. Details may be blurred, but the outlines are surprisingly firm and clear.

The importance of stressing and clarifying Coleridge's method rather than his particular insights must be insisted upon. During recent years criticism has been established once more as a technique to be examined and learned rather than a talent to be used vaguely for minor creations. The progress of modern critical theory has in large part consisted in emphasizing the necessity of analyzing technique, devising better approaches, and formulating more applicable methods. Such an emphasis is of course not new; it is in fact nearly as old as criticism itself. Both Aristotle and Longinus recognized, as clearly as any modern, the need for a defined method, and each consciously used a special technique. The suggestion that no critical approach, no instrument was necessary would have been treated as nonsense by either one.

Exactly that suggestion has been made and often repeated by the impressionists of the last fifty years. Most frequently quoted perhaps is Anatole France's line to the effect that criticism is the adventures of a man's soul in the presence of masterpieces. Such an attitude is obviously a deterrent to the analysis of method and the discriminating use of the laboratory which are essential to both the clarification and the enrichment of critical technique. It may, of course, be argued that an attitude which is a deterrent to one sort of investigation is still of great value in itself. But there is small value in impressionism. The impressionistic critic not only limits himself to the creation of what is at best minor poetry: he expressly negates the existence of the very field in which he is working. But thinking about rather than merely reacting to literature has come into its own. Among a number of critics who are examining method and exploring new possibilities, the most familiar names are I. A. Richards and John Dewey.

When the position that criticism is a technique is accepted, there at once appears as a corollary the fact that, being a technique, criticism is an instrument separable from its users. Methods of approach to literature can be examined and discussed as profitably as can methods of handling a brush or playing a violin. The fact that the examination must always be with strict reference to the end in view in no way invalidates the study of method as method. There is, however, a genuine danger in the present emphasis upon technique; but it is a danger only to those who approach the subject too naïvely. It lies in the unwarranted assumption that critical principles alone are enough; that they will cut into the material as surely when wielded by one hand as by another. Nothing could be more erroneous. The finest critical instrument that ever has been or will be invented carries no guarantee of validity for literary judgments when those judgments are produced by a clumsy or mistaken use of the method. The analogy with the technique of an art holds: a natural aptitude must be present as surely in criticism as in playing a musical instrument. Too worshipful reliance upon principles, an attitude which is a combination of half-knowledge plus intolerance, has produced such curiosities as Rymer's attack upon Shakespeare.

Coleridge had in several respects the ideal equipment for a literary critic: a high order of imaginative power; a craftsman's knowledge of the practical problems confronting a poet; a real delight in and talent for thinking about literature. But although he could begin both to write creatively and to think about literature, he could rarely if ever finish. He once made a remark about Plato which is an excellent description of his own writings: "The sunny mist, the luminous gloom."[1] The maze of critical and speculative material which he left certainly is shrouded in mist and gloom and it is, with equal certainty, both sunny and luminous. Everywhere in him, both in his works and in his personal life, there is lack of system. It is a curious irony that his most valuable contribution to thinking about literature is a theory of criticism which is genuinely structural, in the best sense systematic. His theory is the direct production of a philosophy which explained in terms of organization the nature of a work of art and the nature of the universe as well. An understanding of the system of thought which he inherited and to an extent evolved, together with the constant modifications made upon it by his emotional insights, is unquestionably requisite to a useful knowledge of his theory of criticism.

With Coleridge we are confronted at the outset by a lifelong conflict between his emotions and mind—or his heart and head, as he himself put it. In terms of this conflict he had two impulses, both in existence from early youth, but of unequal duration. The first was poetic, the second speculative. He writes:

At a very premature age, even before my fifteenth year, I had bewildered myself in metaphysics, and in theological controversy. . . . Poetry itself, yea novels and romances became insipid to me. . . . Well were it for me, perhaps, had I never relapsed into the same mental disease; if I had continued to pluck the flower and reap the harvest from the cultivated surface, instead of delving in the unwholesome quicksilver mines of metaphysic depths . . . which exercised the strength and subtlety of the understanding without awakening the feelings of the heart.[2]

---

[1] *Anima Poetae* (cited below as *A.P.*), p. 31.

[2] *Biographia Literaria,* ed. Shawcross (cited below as *B.L.*), Vol. I, p. 9. For similar

The poetic impulse is consistently given a higher place than the speculative; the heart is a better thing than the head. Yet, with reference to his own work, he cannot be accused of a bad emphasis on the "head" because the element of "heart" is consistently prominent in him. He goes out of his way in the *Biographia* to give credit to the mystics Fox, Behmen, and Law for supporting emotion. He writes, "They contributed to keep alive the heart in the head; gave me an indistinct, yet stirring and working presentiment, that all the products of the mere reflective faculty partook of death, and were as the rattling twigs and sprays in winter, into which a sap was yet to be propelled from some root to which I had not penetrated."[3]

The indication is that the heart is fundamentally necessary to philosophical writing. Where his head leads, Coleridge will go only if his emotions are ready to follow. Reasoning divorced from actual experience is worthless to him. Yet ultimately, reason forced under emotional control produces an unacceptable mixture, because obviously intuitions or knowledge which comes under the head of emotional assumptions should be a point of departure for philosophy, rather than a point of arrival or a fence to keep you on the road. Thinking guided by emotions led to the characteristic difficulty of temperament previously mentioned. The conflict between head and heart endured throughout his life; but it was at least partly resolved in the expression of a philosophy in which he was able to use emotion as a means of illuminating a metaphysical principle.

The philosophic scheme which Coleridge has left comes under the general heading of idealism, although he differs in important ways from any other idealistic thinker. A principle common to all idealists is the negation of the reality of the phenomenal world. One result of this principle is that any idealistic system readily

passages, see *A.P.*, p. 3, and particularly p. 164, where he compares himself to Swift: "The pine tree blasted at the top was applied by Swift to himself as a prophetic emblem of his own decay. The chestnut is a fine shady tree, and its wood excellent, were it not that it dies away at the *heart* first."

[3] *B.L.*, Vol. I, p. 98.

lends itself to a spiritual as well as an intellectual interpretation. Coleridge's interest in and use of such a theory was inevitable. An introspective, sensitive child, he was from earliest boyhood drawn to the strange, the marvelous, or the supernatural. At every point in his life we are confronted with this aspect of his mind, whether it be in his private affairs, his poetry, his critical or theological writings. There is no better illustration of this natural bent than in the frequently quoted letter to Poole: "From my early reading of fairy tales and genii etc. my mind had been habituated to the Vast, and I never regarded *my senses* in any way as the criteria of my belief. I regulated all my creeds by my conceptions, not by my sight even at that age."[4]

Given a predisposition so strongly formed and an added love for metaphysics and theological controversy, the growth of some form of idealistic thought became assured. The point I wish to make here is an important one in my treatment of his work as a whole. It is this: The entire range of Coleridge's thought presents a mind which is trying to find a rational philosophic justification for an intuitive emotional belief. Coleridge does not do what is a legitimate thing in philosophy, start with this belief and try to build a system on it, logically supported and continued. Rather, he founds his philosophy on a totally different assumption which he hoped would resolve itself into a proof of the emotional belief which he valued so highly. This assumption, or cardinal principle, from which he starts is the one common to idealistic thought. It is found in the *Sum* or *I Am,* and amounts in short to the act of self-consciousness. The other belief which is really central to Coleridge's conviction is in a one and indivisible unity called God in which man participates. It is his heart that tells him this is true; and when his heart conflicts with his head, so much the worse for intellect: "Believe me Southey! a metaphysical solution that does not instantly tell you something in the heart is grievously to be suspected as apocryphal."[5]

[4] *Letters,* ed. E. H. Coleridge, p. 16.
[5] *Ibid.,* p. 428.

II. UNDERSTANDING AND REASON

A GENUINE KNOWLEDGE of Coleridge's criticism depends fundamentally upon an understanding of his metaphysical speculations. But the connection between his criticism and his metaphysics is rarely obvious and is often extremely obscure. The problem is both to demonstrate and to clarify this relationship. I say demonstrate because of the numerous critics of the past who have denied the importance and even the existence of such a connection. In accomplishing this it will be necessary to take into account formative influences which presented themselves as material with which to justify the belief that was instinctive in him. Perhaps an undue emphasis has been laid upon his debt to German writers, in spite of the frequent similarity between Coleridge's thought and even phrase and theirs in many places. Certain it is that before May, 1799, when he wrote from Germany to Josiah Wedgewood, "I shall have bought thirty pounds worth of books, chiefly metaphysics,"[1] the essentially idealistic nature of his thought was already formed, and that what remained was to amplify and continue rather than originate. We have the evidence of his letters[2] to bear this out, as well as certain passages in the *Biographia.*[3] Charles Lamb has written of the young Coleridge[4] unfolding the mysteries of Iamblichus and Plotinus even before he attended Cambridge. Coleridge himself, referring to the Cambridge period, says,

> But as it was my constant reply to authorities brought against me from later poets of great name, that no authority could avail in opposition to Truth, Nature, Logic, and the Laws of Universal Grammar; actuated too by my former passion for metaphysical investigations; I laboured at a solid foundation on which permanently to ground my opinions, in the com-

---

[1] *Tom Wedgewood,* by R. B. Litchfield, p. 71.

[2] *Letters,* pp. 4–21.

[3] *B.L.,* Vol. I, pp. 3, 9, 14. For similar expressions in Coleridge's verse, see *Coleridge's Poetical Works,* Oxford ed., p. 77, 101, 114.

[4] "Christ's Hospital Five and Thirty Years Ago."

ponent faculties of the human mind itself, and their comparative dignity and importance. According to the faculty or source, from which the pleasure given by any poem or passage was derived, I estimated the merit of such poem or passage.[5]

Although it is true that he does not go on to explain his labors here, the passage gives pretty clear evidence of the nature of his thought before his contact with Germany. Professor Claude Howard, in his book *Coleridge's Idealism,* lays great stress upon the influence of the Cambridge Platonists, Cudworth, Whichcote, and Henry More, with their implied background of Plato and Plotinus. I am in agreement with his summary: "The Platonic thought entered Coleridge's plastic mind early and impressed its indelible mark upon his own naturally idealistic attitude, and the Kantian philosophy aided further in developing and maturing this attitude and then became its instrument."[6]

Because of the lack of an ordered account of Coleridge's intellectual development and the great similarity of ideas found in writers of the Platonic school generally, it is impossible to point with assurance to definite names and works as sources. What is possible is to specify striking and characteristic likenesses between their thought and that of Coleridge.[7]

The most important conception which Coleridge found in the Platonists was that of a transcendental reality existing behind the world of material objects. "I never regarded my senses in any way as the criteria of my belief."[8] His disregard of factual reality endured throughout the whole of his life, if we except the period in which he was dominated by Hartley. The simplest explanation of this "transcendental reality" is that the material world which we see before us is imperfect and changing, that we cannot attach the word "reality" to it; but behind this world there is one which is unchanging and eternal, which possesses the perfection of the faulty world in which we live. In the Cambridge Platonists as

---

[5] *B.L.,* Vol. I, p. 14.   [6] Howard, *Coleridge's Idealism,* p. 100.

[7] It is well to mention at this time that Platonism had received an impetus in England through the translations of Plato made by Thomas Taylor, beginning in 1792.

[8] *Letters,* p. 16. See above, p. 5.

in Plotinus the transcendental world is one and indivisible in its
essence and represents reality, which is God. The natural world,
including man, is derived from God and therefore participates
in the essence. The link between the ideal world and that of ordinary experience is somewhat vaguely conceived, but the fact that
such a link exists is not for a moment doubted. The inclination
of Coleridge to such an explanation is illustrated when he writes:

> The universe itself! what but an immense heap of little things? I can
> contemplate nothing but *parts* and *parts* are all little. My mind feels as if
> it ached to behold and know something *great*, something *one* and *indi-
> visible*. And it is only in the faith of that, that rocks or waterfalls, moun-
> tains or caverns give me the sense of sublimity or majesty! But in this faith
> *all things* counterfeit infinity.[9]

Here he frankly falls back on faith to support a belief in the ideal
world. It was not until later that he made such a world an object
of knowledge through what he termed "reason."

There can be little doubt that the appeal of this system was
largely to his emotions and imagination, and there is some reason
to believe that Coleridge himself could not at the time see a real
justification for it. He speaks of Plato's "gorgeous nonsense,"[10] his
"sunny mist" and "luminous gloom."[11] But the emotional appeal,
justifiably or not, was the most real to him, and as a result the
shadow of a loose idealism is cast over the whole of his thought.

The second important conception which may be traced back
to the Platonists lies in Coleridge's distinction between the understanding and the reason, conceived of as faculties of the mind. It
is a distinction with which he was greatly concerned in his philosophical thought; from its formulation he derived the distinction
between imagination and fancy as stated in the *Biographia*. In
Table Talk he says, "Until you have mastered the fundamental
difference in kind, between the reason and the understanding as
faculties of the human mind, you cannot escape a thousand difficulties in philosophy."[12] *The Friend*, his first philosophical work,

---

[9] *Letters*, p. 228.   [11] *A.P.*, p. 31.
[10] *Ibid.*, p. 211.   [12] *Table Talk*, ed. H. N. Coleridge, 1847, p. 72.

contains a statement of the meaning of the terms. Following Kant's *Critique of Pure Reason,* he makes a "threefold distinction in human nature," namely, sense, understanding, and reason. He continues:

> Under the term sense, I comprise whatever is passive in our being. . . . all that man is in common with the animals, in kind at least—his sensations and impressions, whether of his outward senses, or the inner sense of imagination. By understanding, I mean the faculty of thinking and forming judgments on the notices furnished by the sense, according to certain rules existing in itself, which rules constitute its distinct nature. By the pure reason, I mean the power by which we become possessed of principles—the eternal verities of Plato and Descartes, and of ideas, not images.[18]

These distinctly Kantian lines are immediately qualified by a statement which, pushed to its conclusion, allies him with the Platonists rather than Kant: "To my readers it will, I trust, be some recommendation of these distinctions, that they were more than once expressed, and everywhere supposed, in the writings of St. Paul."[14]

Confronted as we are by a confusion of Kant and the Platonists, it is necessary to make very clear the part which each plays. The Neo-Platonic psychology was dualistic, being concerned with sense on the one hand and understanding *or* reason on the other. The two latter terms were used interchangeably. By "sense" they meant sensations or impressions. The distinction between the Platonic and Kantian "sense" is irrelevant at the moment. The difficulty lies in the "reason." To state the case broadly, we have the Platonists regarding reason as a faculty by which man can have knowledge of God; and the knowledge is constitutive, a part of reality, and becomes unified with faith rather than abrogates the need of it. It means, in short, that God is knowable intellectually as well as emotionally. To Kant, such a position was impossible, for only phenomena were knowable. Reason as a faculty could not possess objects of knowledge; it could merely regulate them. So the idea of God is a postulate, regulative and not consti-

---

[18] *The Friend,* ed. Shedd, p. 164.   [14] *Ibid.*

tutive. But although we are unable to prove God's existence, since he is not an object of knowledge, it is equally impossible to disprove it. This is Kant's final stand.

Reason for the Platonists becomes not only a faculty of the human mind reaching toward God, but also an emanation coming from God to mankind, in which man may participate because he is created in God's image. Benjamin Whichcote, an early member of the Cambridge group, writes, "Reverence God in thyself: for God is more in the Mind of Man than in any part of this world besides; for we are made after the image of God."[15] The connection between reason and God is made by Ralph Cudworth: "Reason is not a shallow thing; it is the first participation from God."[16] In another passage, "To go against reason is to go against God; it is the self same to do that which the reason of the case doth require, and that which God doth himself appoint. Reason is the divine Governor of man's life; it is the very voice of God."[17] Nathanael Culverwell uses a favorite figure when he holds that "... the understanding alone is the Candle of the Lord.... By this candle of the Lord, Adam and Eve discovered their own folly and nakedness; this Candle flamed in Cain's conscience, and this law was proclaimed in the heart with as much terror, as 'twas published from Mount Sinai, which filled him with furious reflections for his unnatural murder."[18]

In the earlier divines, Hooker and Leighton, there are passages which suggest a similar conception of the functions of reason and understanding, although the distinctions are not fully worked out and the terminology is inexact. The two terms are used synonymously, but it is made evident that there is one faculty of the mind which deals with the materials furnished by sense (the understanding, for Coleridge) and another faculty which has knowledge of God. Coleridge takes John Smith as an illustration of the fact that the distinction has "been asserted by many both

[15] Campagnac, *The Cambridge Platonists*, p. 70.   [17] *Ibid.*, p. 100.
[16] Tulloch, *Rational Theology in England*, p. 110.   [18] Campagnac, *op. cit.*, p. 213.

before and since Lord Bacon."[19] He quotes Smith: "While we reflect upon our own idea of Reason, we know that our souls are not in it, but only partake of it;...Neither can it be called a faculty, but far rather a light...the source of which is not within ourselves, nor rightly by any individual to be denominated *mine*. This pure intelligence [Coleridge continues] he then proceeds to contrast with the discursive faculty, that is, the understanding."[20] The foregoing will be sufficient, I believe, to demonstrate that the distinction of functions existed in the earlier writers and was known by Coleridge.[21]

In Kant, facultative psychology becomes closely and logically delineated. The mind has three faculties: sense, understanding, and reason. The understanding deals with the phenomena furnished by sense, and it is this material only which can become an object of knowledge. The ultimate source of the world is unknowable; we can deal with nothing but appearances. However, our knowledge here is constitutive, because the structure of the understanding operating on the sense manifold constitutes phenomena. These phenomena are the objects of scientific knowledge. Reason gives us our ideas of freedom, immortality, and God; but since these are in the realm of the supersensuous they can never become objects of knowledge; they must remain regulative, not susceptible of proof, because they are beyond human experience. The result is that the existence of God can be neither proved nor disproved.

It becomes apparent that Coleridge has merged the Platonic and Kantian conceptions of reason. Bearing in mind the passage

[19] *Works,* ed. Shedd, Vol. I, p. 264.

[20] *Ibid.*

[21] Coleridge once defined reason in rhyme:
> "When'er the mist that stands 'twixt God and thee
> Defecates to a pure transparency,
> That intercepts no light and adds no stain—
> There Reason is and there begins her reign."
> (*Poetical Works,* Oxford ed., p. 487)

For a more lengthy discussion of reason and understanding see *The Friend,* ed. Shedd, pp. 137–150.

from *The Friend* already quoted[22] which has a distinct savor of Kant, I should like to place beside it another:

> I should have no objection to define reason with Jacobi ... as an organ bearing the same relation to spiritual objects, the universal, the eternal and the necessary, as the eye bears to material and contingent phenomena. But then it must be added that it is an organ identical with its appropriate objects. Thus, God, the soul, eternal truth, etc. are the objects of reason; but they are themselves reason. ... [Reason] has the power of acquainting itself with invisible realities or spiritual objects.[23]

It is significant that Jacobi realized the situation more clearly than Coleridge and took sharp issue with Kant (asserting that only through faith could we know God). Coleridge, however, goes where Jacobi will not and extends the definition, making reason identical with God. Here he is the descendant of the Cambridge Platonists quoted before. But this is not enough. In the *Biographia,* he does Kant the favor of making excuses for him, saying, "The apparent contradictions which occur, I soon found were hints and insinuations referring to ideas, which Kant either did not think it prudent to avow, or which he considered as consistently left behind in a pure analysis ... of the speculative intellect alone."[24] What these insinuations were, is left for the reader to discover for himself; Coleridge never enlightens him.

The conclusion of the matter now becomes clear. Judging from the use which Coleridge makes of the Kantian distinctions, we see he must have realized that they were logically far more valid than those explicit or implicit in the writings of the earlier Platonists. Yet there is a barrier to his acceptance of Kant, one which is profoundly significant in a study of his works as a whole. For Kant, a logical conclusion about the existence of God is impossible for human beings because the subject is beyond human knowledge. If we accept Kant's premises and then hold that God is knowable, the whole system will fall to pieces. This was Coleridge's problem, the old affair of the head versus the heart. His solution was thoroughly characteristic of him. The small chance

---

[22] See above, p. 9.   [23] *The Friend,* ed. Shedd, p. 144.   [24] *B.L.,* Vol. I, p. 99.

which the intellect had of victory over the emotions is indicated by his explanation of Kant as making "hints and insinuations" referring to ideas. In spite of the salty palate and strong stomach which one must have to swallow such a mixture, he accepted Kant and then made God an object of knowledge. When Coleridge's mind and emotions were at war, the result was, perhaps, a foregone conclusion. But if the metaphysical system of Kant lay in ruins about him, this was by no means true of the Platonists. Weakness of proof becomes immaterial when a strong emotional faith has already decided the issue. So with regard to the understanding and reason, Kant must be given credit for the formal distinction, the Platonists for the real substance. We are reminded of the line, "A metaphysical solution that does not instantly tell you something in the heart is grievously to be suspected as apocryphal."[25] Coleridge's thought was always subject to approval by his emotions, and his greatest emotional need was for a real and knowable God.

Yet in spite of Coleridge's "correction" of Kant, he looked upon that philosopher as one who possessed true greatness. In the *Biographia* he writes: "[The works of Kant] took possession of me as with a giant's hand. After fifteen years' familiarity with them, I still read these and all his other productions with undiminished delight and increasing admiration."[26] Schlegel and Schelling he looked upon as equals, Kant as a superior.

[25] *Letters*, p. 428. See above, p. 5.

[26] *B.L.*, Vol. I, p. 99.

III. IMAGINATION AND FANCY

IT IS ONLY in view of Coleridge's discussion of understanding and reason that we can approach his distinction between imagination and fancy. Shawcross has shown, in his essay on Coleridge, that from his early years Coleridge felt rather than perceived a difference between the two. In the *Biographia* Coleridge relates how the recital of a poem by Wordsworth led him "... to suspect that fancy and imagination were two distinct and widely different faculties, instead of being, according to the general belief, either two names with one meaning, or at furthest, the lower and higher degree of one and the same power."[1] It is significant that he remarks that what impressed him most was "... the original gift of spreading the tone, the atmosphere, and with it the depth and height of the ideal world around forms, incidents and situations."[2] The incident spoken of took place in 1796 before he had come into contact with German philosophy; however, since the account was written about 1814, it is of no value except so far as it demonstrates the early presence in his mind of the distinction.

That such a distinction did exist in a vague and somewhat inarticulate form before his acquaintance with Kant, can hardly be doubted. It must be remembered that Coleridge referred to him at that time as the "most unintelligible Immanuel Kant."[3] That attitude was soon changed, for his studies in the critical philosophy during the years 1801–1806 resulted in the lifelong admiration for Kant which I have mentioned before. It is natural, then, that at the time he was writing the *Biographia,* having already used, or perhaps misused, the Kantian distinctions of sense, understanding, and reason, he should look to Kant for a logical description of the function of the imagination. It is also natural that, placing as he did the highest value upon feeling, he should agree only partly with Kant, who was inclined to discount the emotional side of our nature. At any rate, he found in Kant an account

---

[1] *B.L.*, Vol. I, p. 59.   [2] *Ibid.*   [3] *Letters*, p. 204.

of imagination which served to orient his own ideas.[4] In the *Critique of Pure Reason*, there is assigned to imagination the function of connecting the understanding, as a purely intellectual faculty, with the sense manifold. In virtue of its twofold nature, the imagination presents that manifold in a form suitable for its subsumption under the categories. Thus the imagination is not a mere faculty of images, or of poetic invention: its peculiar characteristic lies in the power of figurative synthesis, or of delineating the forms of things in general. Moreover, in performing this function it is subject to the laws of the understanding: its procedure, therefore, contributes nothing to our knowledge of the origin of phenomena. But for this very reason of its conformity to the understanding, its deliverances are objective, that is, valid for all thinking beings; and are in this respect to be distinguished from the creations of its reproductive activity, which as subject to empirical conditions (the laws of association) have merely individual and contingent validity. Finally, in the aesthetic judgment, the imagination, though still receiving its law from the understanding, is yet so far free, that its activity is determined not by the necessity of a particular cognition, but by its own character as an organ of knowledge in general.

Kant thus distinguishes three functions or activities of the imagination: as reproductive, in which it is subject to empirical conditions; as productive, in which it acts spontaneously and determines phenomena instead of being determined by them, but yet in accordance with a law of the understanding; and as aesthetic, when it attains its highest degree of freedom in respect of the object, which it regards as material for a possible, not an actual and impending, act of cognition.[5]

Turning now to Coleridge's treatment of the subject, we find both similarities and differences. In Chapter Thirteen of the

---

[4] For material on the relation of Kant and Schelling to Coleridge I am largely indebted to Shawcross' essay published as a preface to the *Biographia*. I am in agreement with and have followed his account of Kant's theory of imagination.

[5] Shawcross' account of Kant's theory of the imagination. *B.L.*, Vol. I, p. lvii.

Biographia he gives his definition of imagination and fancy. It is worth remarking that the chapter begins with an extremely confused metaphysical discussion which suddenly breaks off, to be followed by a letter from a friend, begging him not to go on. Since the letter was written by Coleridge to himself, he must have found the advice very easy to accept. At any rate, he discontinues the discussion and suddenly presents the result to the reader, saying that he has reserved the full paper for future publication. Because of its importance I am quoting the definition in full:

> The *imagination* then, I consider either as primary or secondary. The primary imagination I hold to be the living Power and prime Agent of all human Perception, and as a repetition in the finite mind of the eternal act of creation in the infinite I AM. The *secondary imagination* I consider as an echo of the former, co-existing with the conscious will yet still as identical with the primary in the kind of its agency, and differing only in degree, and in the mode of its operation. It dissolves, diffuses, dissipates, in order to recreate; or where this process is rendered impossible, yet still at all events it struggles to idealize and to unify. It is essentially *vital,* even as all objects (as objects) are essentially fixed and dead.
>
> *Fancy,* on the contrary, has no other counters to play with, but fixities and definites. The fancy is indeed no other than a mode of Memory emancipated from the order of time and space; while it is blended with, and modified by that empirical phenomenon of the will, which we express by the word CHOICE. But equally with the ordinary memory the Fancy must receive all its materials ready made from the law of association.[6]

It will be seen that there is a correspondence between the reproductive imagination of Kant and the fancy of Coleridge. For Kant, the imagination in its reproductive activity was subject to empirical conditions and so had merely individual and contingent validity; it lacked the universal validity of the productive imagination as well as the freedom of the imagination in the aesthetic judgment. For Coleridge, fancy played "with fixities and definites." It was merely a mode of memory guided by choice. It was entirely a result of empirical conditions which meant association. Coleridge's definition is merely the adaptation and articulation of the feeling he had many years before when he heard

---

[6] *B.L.,* Vol. I, p. 202.

Wordsworth read a poem and was impressed for the first time with the difference between dealing in artificial, dead combinations and infusing into material a living power to which he gave the name imagination.

The productive imagination of Kant has some relation to the primary imagination of Coleridge, although not so close a one as the reproductive has to fancy. As a universal factor in knowledge it was by far the more important to Kant. It will be remembered that the productive imagination mediated between the understanding and the sense manifold; but inasmuch as it conformed to the laws of the understanding, that particular sort of imagination attained objectivity, becoming universally valid for thinking beings. This was a new conception to Coleridge, who had always looked upon imagination as a special gift possessed by the favored few, rather than as a universal faculty. Yet the theory must have been singularly attractive to him, since it was his purpose to discover laws which were universally valid. It is not too much to say that Kant's distinction enlarged Coleridge's idea so that he came to recognize two degrees of imagination: the first, universal for all mankind ("the primary imagination I hold to be the living power and prime agent of all human perception");[7] and the second, the gift owned by those with the greatest insight. Although the logic of the passage on secondary imagination points otherwise, the applications elsewhere invariably show that it is possessed only by the exceptional man.

Coleridge's concept of secondary imagination goes back for its origin to those vague, emotional stirrings of his youth in which he felt the power, life, and beauty of the universe, and embedded them in certain of his poems without being able to fit them into a philosophical system.[8] The difference between his secondary and Kant's aesthetic imagination is more striking than the similarity. Coleridge elevated the secondary imagination to a posi-

[7] *Ibid.* See above, p. 16.

[8] "Effusion at Evening," *Poetical Works* (Oxford ed.), p. 49; "Lines on a Friend," *ibid.*, p. 76; "The Eolian Harp," *ibid.*, p. 100; "Religious Musings," *ibid.*, p. 108; "The Destiny of Nations," *ibid.*, p. 131; "Ode to the Departing Year," *ibid.*, p. 160.

tion of far greater significance than Kant could allow. For Kant, the aesthetic imagination rested in the recognition of the harmony of the faculties of knowledge in view of any particular object; it must have the highest degree of freedom in respect of the object. But the greatest drawback which Coleridge felt in Kant is reminiscent of his interpretation of Kant's reason, namely, that the aesthetic imagination had no warranty in the supersensuous field. Its activity was formal only; it could tell nothing of the real ground of things. An emotional rather than an intellectual necessity forced Coleridge to go beyond Kant in search of a system which would support the requirements of his feelings. The subjectivity of Kant, universally shared by mankind though it might be, was yet too insubstantial. Coleridge is everywhere consistent in his belief that the ultimate ground of reality contains in itself the possibility of being known by the reason. It follows, then, that because this reality is manifested in both man and nature the forming activity of the imagination has objective truth and depends ultimately upon the validity of the reason knowing. Thus the reason knows, but the imagination illuminates and reveals that knowledge.

It becomes apparent that Kant does little to explain the real nature of Coleridge's definition of the imagination. That explanation must be sought in two other German philosophers, Fichte and Schelling. Coleridge, in the account of his philosophical studies in the *Biographia,* writes:

Fichte's *Wissenschaftslehre* or *Lore of Ultimate Science,* was to add the keystone of the arch; and by commencing with an *act,* instead of a thing or substance . . . supplied the idea of a system truly metaphysical and a metaphysic truly systematic. . . . But this fundamental idea he overbuilt with a heavy mass of mere notions, and psychological acts of arbitrary reflection. Thus his theory degenerated into a crude egoismus, a boastful and hyper-stoic hostility to nature, as lifeless, godless, and altogether unholy.[9]

He continues with a consideration of his obligations to Schelling, saying, "In Schelling's *Natur-Philosophie* and the *System des*

[9] *B.L.,* Vol. I, p. 101.

transcendentalen Idealismus I first found a genial coincidence with much that I had toiled out for myself, and a powerful assistance in what I have yet to do."[10] He defends himself against plagiarism with the statement that not even an identity of thought or a similarity of phrase is certain proof that he has borrowed. He pays the highest compliments to Schelling as the founder of the philosophy of nature, but avers that the most striking resemblances and all the fundamental ideas were born and matured in his mind before he had ever seen a single page of Schelling. His explanation is that they were both of the same school, both outgrowths of the same sources. A conclusion is brought to the matter, which, perhaps, contains as much logic as Coleridge was able to evolve. He writes, "I regard truth as a divine ventriloquist: I care not from whose mouth the sounds are supposed to proceed, if only the words are audible and intelligible."[11] His defense is in some degree justifiable, although his contention that Schelling's system was already matured in his mind when he first read him will hardly stand scrutiny; it has been shown that in many places Coleridge has simply translated parts of Schelling and offered the result as his own.[12] He was, however, notoriously lax in his system of keeping notes, and it is within the bounds of possibility that, in looking over material taken sometime before, he may have confused his original thoughts with notes taken on Schelling or even direct translations made from him. The important thing at the moment is the presence of the indebtedness, rather than its exact measure.

In order to understand the nature of this influence, I should like to consider for a moment the philosophical position of Fichte and Schelling.[13] Both of these men may be regarded as philosophers of romanticism, Schelling in particular. The objection raised to Kant by the romantic philosophers in general was that totality,

---

[10] *Ibid.*   [11] *Ibid.*, p. 105.

[12] See *Biographia Literaria*, ed. H. N. Coleridge, 1847, Appendix.

[13] The best general but compact account of this material is in Höffding's *History of Modern Philosophy*.

the conception of a whole, was lacking. They felt that a system was needed which would embrace the whole content of spiritual life, and that such a system would be best if deduced from a single absolute principle. This approach was sharply different from that of Kant, who assumed that knowledge presupposed something outside itself which always escaped us; that is, the thing-in-itself. If this very important assumption were abandoned, there would be no objection to a logical construction of philosophy starting from Kant's thought of synthesis as the essence of spirit. According to Höffding:

> All externality, isolation, and division would disappear from spiritual life if the unity of things were thus exhibited, if all forms of life could be shown to be degrees and phases of the same infinite life which lives in all of them. In this way not only the conscious life of individual men, but also the historical life of the race, and, by the method of analogy, the life of Nature would be shown in a new light. And we should thus obtain an explanation not merely of one side of the spiritual life of man; if the guiding principle were conceived in all its depth it must lead beyond the existing separation between knowledge, religion and art, and reconcile all discords of the spirit.[14]

Fichte, generally regarded as Kant's disciple, is a member of the group called philosophers of romanticism. Like them, he emphasized the independence, validity, and inwardness of spiritual life. He called his system "idealism." It was his task in *Wissenschafts-lehre* to show that our ideas of things are produced by the activity of thought assigning definite limits in accordance with its nature. His assumption is that there can be nothing in the ego which is not a product of the ego's own activity. He reverses the order of Kant, who had begun with the sense manifold and worked back to an all-embracing unity, by starting from the original activity of the ego and attempting to deduce from it the special forms of the manifold. There are two elements in his philosophy which are of importance for us with relation to Coleridge: first, he starts with an act rather than a fact; second, this act contains within itself the necessity for progression—it is dynamic. His method has

[14] *Op. cit.,* Vol. II, p. 140.

been called antithetical: first, a proposition is asserted which brings out a moment of truth; then follows a second proposition which expresses an opposite moment, which cannot be deduced from the first; finally, we attain a union of the two. The necessity for the union is contained in the first principle, that everything in consciousness is due to an indivisible spiritual activity, for it follows from this that the relation of opposition cannot be fundamental. The method is fully developed, each synthesis becoming in turn a thesis, to be combined with a new antithesis which forms a new synthesis.

The first element in Fichte which I mentioned, his beginning with an act, Coleridge uses in the *Biographia,* giving Fichte credit for supplying the "keystone of the arch." The second gave him the idea of a system dynamic, progressive, and spiritual. It was for such a system that Coleridge was searching, but unless it contained a knowable supersensuous reality he could not accept it. This, Fichte could not give him, so he condemns Fichte's system as a "crude egoismus, a boastful and hyper-stoic hostility to nature, as lifeless, godless, and altogether unholy."[15] What Coleridge desired was, as the ground of reality, a spirit which was God, revealing itself both in man and in the forms of nature according to discernible laws.

For a time it seemed to him that he had found this in Schelling. Fichte had made nature merely a limit or a means; it was object only. In Schelling, however, he found an interpretation of it as a manifestation of spirit. Schelling's contention was that it could be understood only if it bore the stamp of spirit. His solution was that the same duality of an infinite and limiting force which Fichte had shown in consciousness must pervade the whole of nature. Since conscious life rests on contradiction (doubleness), the whole of nature, out of which conscious life develops, must exhibit opposing forces, but at lower powers. Matter is slumbering spirit, spirit in equilibrium; and spirit is matter in process of becoming. But the important problem is to trace the stages by

---

[15] *B.L.,* Vol. I, p. 101. See above, p. 18.

which nature rises to spirit. In these stages the forces and forms of nature are conceived of as forming progressively graduated approximations to conscious life. Each stage contains within itself a moment of contradiction appearing in consciousness under the form of subject and object (the ego and the nonego).

The absolute principle or original ground which underlies all things contains the absolute unity of subject and object. Although this unity is never annulled, object or subject may preponderate quantitatively. In nature the objective, in spirit the subjective preponderates. There are three powers of the spirit: knowledge, action, and art. Artistic intuition, or imagination, is the highest form of spiritual life. Art authenticates what philosophy cannot exhibit externally, that is, the unconscious in action and production, and its original identity with the conscious. Art reveals in unity that which is separate or torn apart in nature, history, life, and action. It discovers the inner ground of harmony between apparent contradictions and thus achieves the highest dignity and importance in the system. In doing so it reflects the ultimate ground of knowledge. This is the highest degree of imagination. There is, however, a lower one, for the imagination is identical in kind with the activity which it contemplates. That is, the original act whereby pure intelligence objectifies and limits itself in order to contemplate itself in its limitation is an act of imagination; this act is common to all mankind, being repeated in the experience of every individual in becoming conscious of the world. But as we rise in self-knowledge the faculty becomes more intense and is only the property of very gifted minds.

In *Transcendental Idealism* Schelling writes: "It is the poetic faculty, which in its first power is the original intuition, and contrariwise, it is only the productive intuition reasserting itself in the highest power, that we call the poetic faculty. It is one and the same power which is active in both, the sole power whereby we are able to think and comprehend what is contradictory—namely, the imagination."[16] Doubtless Schelling's conception of

---

[16] Schelling, *Werke*, 1858, Bd. III, p. 626.

the imagination as reconciling opposites and so underlying all acts of knowledge was a development of Kant's description in which the imagination mediates between the understanding and the sense manifold; but whatever the logical validity of Schelling may be, he has gone far beyond Kant in conceiving the imagination as recognizing the inherent interdependence of subject and object. Imagination is the organ of philosophy in the sense that philosophy must start from a fundamental experience and that the imagination makes that experience possible. The experience is given outwardly in the products of art.

With this account of Schelling in mind I should like to turn to the passage in the *Biographia* which leads up to the chapter on imagination. Coleridge here makes an attempt to state his system and from it "to deduce the memory with all the other functions of intelligence." Actually the promise is never fulfilled; he views his system only in connection with the imagination, and even there he gives up the attempt to explain and merely states the definition.

Coleridge's system is as follows. There are two factors: the objective, by which he means nature in the passive sense, the external world; and the subjective, which is self or intelligence. Knowledge depends upon an identity of subject with object; but in the act of knowledge the two factors are so mixed that we cannot tell to which one priority belongs. Therefore there are two possibilities: either the objective is taken first, that is, as a starting place for a metaphysics, and then we have to account for the supervention of the subjective; or the subjective is taken first, and the problem is to account for the supervention to it of a coincident objective. Taking up the first possibility, he says that the highest perfection of natural philosophy would consist in the perfect spiritualization of all the laws of nature into laws of intellect and intuition. As the principle of law breaks forth, the phenomena themselves become more spiritual and at length cease altogether in our consciousness."[17] So far he has been paraphrasing

---

[17] *B.L.*, Chap. XII.

Schelling,[18] although perhaps unconsciously. But here a significant difference appears. Schelling writes:

> The perfected theory of nature would be that in virtue of which all nature should resolve itself into an intelligence: The dead and unconscious products of nature are only abortive attempts of nature to reflect herself; but the so-called DEAD nature in general is an unripe intelligence; thence through her phenomena, even while yet unconscious, the intelligent character discovers itself.[19]

Coleridge's version is,

> ... the theory of natural philosophy would then be completed when all nature was demonstrated to be identical in essence with that which in its highest power exists in man as intelligence and self-consciousness, when the heavens and the earth shall declare not only the power of their Maker, but the glory and the presence of their God, even as he appeared to the great prophet during the vision of the mount in the skirts of his divinity.[20]

A comparison of these two passages makes it clear that while Coleridge is following Schelling, he is not doing so slavishly; that his head is still attentive to the demands of his heart and that those demands include a real and knowable God. In this comparison there is the seed of his final repudiation of Schelling.

Coleridge continues with the second possibility, that of taking the subjective first. If we start with I AM, the assumption is groundless, but only because it is the ground of all other possibility. The converse proposition, namely, that the existence of external nature should be received as blindly as the existence of our own being, can only be solved by the transcendental philosopher by the assumption that the former is unconsciously involved in the latter; that it is not only coherent, but identical, and one and the same thing with our own immediate self-consciousness. Here again he is paraphrasing Schelling. Coleridge then endeavors to demonstrate the truth of the assumption by a series of theses. His argument runs as follows. Truth is correlative to being; knowledge without a correspondent of reality is no knowledge. All truth is either mediate, that is, derived from other

---

[18] Schelling, *Werke*, Bd. I, pp. 338–342.
[19] *Op. cit.*, Bd. I, p. 342.   [20] *B.L.*, Vol. I, p. 176.

truth, or else immediate and original. The latter is absolute, the former dependent and conditional. We are to seek, then, for some absolute truth capable of giving certainty to other positions. This truth must be of a nature to preclude the possibility of requiring a cause or antecedent. There can be only one such principle. This cannot be a thing or object, because each object is what it is in consequence of some other object. This principle manifests itself in the SUM or I AM, which is to be designated by the words "spirit" or "self-consciousness." In this, subject and object, being and knowing, are identical, each involving and supposing the other. It may be described as a perpetual self-duplication of one and the same power into object and subject, which presuppose each other and can exist only as *antitheses*. If we elevate our conception to the absolute self, the great eternal I AM, then the principles of being and of knowledge, of idea and reality, are absolutely identical. Spirit, which is originally the identity of subject and object, must in some sense dissolve this identity, in order to become conscious of it. This implies an act and it follows, therefore, that self-consciousness is impossible except by and in a will. In the existence, the reconciling and recurring of the antitheses, consists the process and mystery of production and life. Consciousness as thus described is, in its various phases, a self-development of absolute spirit or intelligence. It works under two opposite and counteracting forces. The intelligence in the one tends to objectize itself, and in the other to know itself in the object. Coleridge concludes by saying:

It will be hereafter my business to construct by a series of intuitions the progressive schemes, that must follow from such a power with such forces, till I arrive at the fullness of the human intelligence. For my present purpose, I assume such a power as my principle, in order to deduce from it a faculty, the generation, agency, and application of which form the contents of the ensuing chapter.[21]

This promise was never fulfilled. The system, such as it is, failed to receive the elaboration which Coleridge intended to bestow.

---

[21] *Ibid.*, pp. 180–188.

The general nature of his obligation to Schelling is pretty clear. First in Fichte, and then in Schelling's *System of Transcendental Idealism,* he found the arguments for the supremacy of the spirit which I have related. But where Fichte failed to give him the conception of a spirit which is inherent in nature, Schelling contained exactly what he was looking for. By the time Coleridge read Schelling he was settled at least in the object of his search. He desired an account of the universe in which spirit was supreme; this spirit must emanate from God and be participated in by man and nature, thus constituting the total unity which Coleridge perceived emotionally but was never able to state in a satisfactory manner.

Faulty though Schelling may have been in his logic, his system established the supremacy of spirit for those who wished to believe in it. At the time Coleridge studied Schelling he was himself engaged in aesthetic problems; so at first a poetic interpretation of the universe such as that philosopher gave seemed to have reached absolute truth. But there is good reason to believe that Coleridge never entirely agreed with Schelling, although he did not formulate his objections in detail. The chaotic, unfinished form of the chapter on imagination can hardly be dismissed with the usual explanation of inability to pursue a subject to its logical conclusion. Perhaps such an inability played its part there, but there is another aspect which demands our attention. In the statement of his system preliminary to his explanation of the imagination, Coleridge had leaned very heavily on Schelling, or at least had shown remarkable similarities to him. If he accepted Schelling entirely, there is no good reason why he could not have continued his borrowing or similarity in his explanation of the imagination. The material was ready to his hand, and he had never shown puritanical scruples about appropriating the work of others. But here he failed to do so and in that failure implied a disagreement with certain features of Schelling. The reason is not hard to find. However obscure the details of Coleridge's thought may be, the larger elements are consistently present. Unquestionably, for him the most unsatisfactory part of Schelling's system was the vague conception of the ultimate ground of reality. In Schelling, the absolute was a mere selfless identity or total indifference, prior to and behind self-consciousness, which was neither subject nor object, but the mere negation of both. With reference to such an abstract principle, the connection of subject and object became a mere matter of logical necessity. There was no place for the God of Coleridge's faith as a "Being in whom reason and a most holy will are one with an infinite power." In the theses of the *Biographia* there can be read Coleridge's effort to identify Schelling's "intellectual intuition" of subject and object in their absolute identity with the religious intuition, the direct consciousness of God. A second and less obvious dissatisfaction which I believe he found in Schelling will be discussed later.

If now we recall Coleridge's definition of the primary imagination ("the living Power and prime Agent of all human Perception, and as a repetition in the finite mind of the eternal act of creation in the infinite I AM")[22] we see a pretty clear echo of Schelling's lower form of imagination, that is, the original act of consciousness whereby it objectifies and limits itself in order to contemplate itself in its limitation. Coleridge's use of the word "power" is significant. For Schelling, imagination was one of the powers of the spirit; for Coleridge, it is the living power of human perception. Apparently it is the spirit or self, expressed in its antithetical working in human perception. The second clause—"and as a repetition in the finite mind of the eternal act of creation in the infinite I AM"—seems to justify this. Imagination in this sense must be common to all mankind. It is creative in that it externalizes the world of objects by opposing it to the self.

The secondary imagination, Coleridge defines as:

... an echo of the former, co-existing with the conscious will, yet still as identical with the primary in the kind of its agency, and differing only in degree, and in the mode of its operation. It dissolves, diffuses, dissipates, in order to recreate; or where this progress is rendered impossible, yet still

[22] *B.L.*, Vol. I, p. 202. See above, p. 16.

at all events it struggles to idealize and to unify. It is essentially vital, even as all objects (as objects) are essentially fixed and dead.[23]

I take this to mean that it is the same faculty as the first only in a heightened power. By the first our exercise of the power is unconsciousness; by the second, the will directs, but does not determine, the activity of the imagination. It is different in degree, that is, owing to its difference it becomes the faculty of poetic minds, the favored few, whereas the primary imagination is common to all men. I should like to have Coleridge's explanation of the words "dissolves, diffuses, dissipates," for I believe that there is contained in those words a difference from the system by which the imagination of Schelling worked. Coleridge's phrase "or where this process is rendered impossible" is incomprehensible to me unless he means that the degree of imagination is not sufficiently high to see the inner harmony. If we assume that the primary imagination is the act of self-consciousness which causes man to see as external to himself those objects which in truth are a modification of his own being, then the secondary imagination is the power by which man reconstructs these objects out of the ideas of his consciousness. Thus the secondary imagination becomes the faculty of mediate vision which embodies in works of art the inner harmony of the world.

The imagination is an essential part of the structure of the universe; it is dynamic, vital. Through its primary degree all mankind is enabled to achieve the act of consciousness involved in the I AM. Through its secondary degree, the artist, the man of great perception, can see through the opposition or contradiction in the world and bring to it reconciliation, synthesis, or unity. Under this system there can be no such thing as pure evil; there is nothing essentially queer, irrational, or inexplicable in the world, for the universe is governed by an inflexible system. What appears to be evil is merely an unresolved opposition which is, nevertheless, working its way toward resolution. The power

[23] *B.L.,* Vol. I, p. 202.

of the secondary or higher imagination brings synthesis to the conflict.

Fancy, it will now be seen, is an entirely different thing in kind. It is not dynamic or vital. It does not come to grips with the essential structure of the universe. By means of "... that empirical phenomenon of the will, which we express by the word CHOICE," it plays with "fixities and definites," in other words, with things which are dead. It is a mode of memory and must receive its materials "ready made from the law of association." When fancy brings two elements together, the union is an unnatural one and lacks significance. When the imagination does the same thing, it reveals a part of the essential order in the world. Coleridge characterizes Milton as having an imaginative, Cowley a fanciful mind.[24] The importance of the distinction cannot be too strongly emphasized. Imagination involves one kind of activity, fancy another kind; that is, the difference is certainly not one of degree— a point which various critics have failed to recognize. The ideas involved in this distinction are implicit in most of Coleridge's critical remarks.[25]

---

[24] *Ibid.*, p. 62. For other passages dealing specifically with the imagination see Raysor, *Coleridge's Shakespearean Criticism*, Vol. II, pp. 212, 216; *A.P.*, p. 236.

[25] For a vigorous support of this point based on psychological rather than metaphysical grounds, see I. A. Richards, *Coleridge on Imagination*, Chap. II, esp. pp. 31–40.

IV. ORGANIC UNITY

AT FIRST GLANCE, Coleridge's definition of imagination does not look very promising as an instrument for literary criticism. During the century which has passed since his death little if any practical use has been made of it. In general, it has been customary to separate his philosophy from his criticism as if the two lacked vital or significant connection. He has been praised repeatedly for the acuteness of his critical remarks, and condemned (although less often) for the amorphous state of his philosophy. For instance, Professor Saintsbury writes, "Coleridge is just so much the more barren in true criticism as he expatiates further in the regions of sheer philosophy."[1] Although he admits the "inextricable entanglement"[2] of philosophy with criticism proper, his summary of Coleridge leaves the two branches separate. I wish to remark, however, that this attitude has been by no means universal. J. Shawcross in his introduction to the *Biographia*, A. E. Powell in her chapter on Coleridge in *A Romantic Theory of Poetry*, and Alice Snyder in *The Critical Principle of the Reconciliation of Opposites as Employed by Coleridge* have all done valuable and suggestive work in linking the literary criticism of Coleridge with his philosophy. Perhaps the most stimulating and most immediately interesting work by any member of this group is I. A. Richards' *Coleridge on Imagination*.[3] The

---

[1] *History of Criticism*, Vol. III, p. 142.   [2] *Ibid.*, p. 169.

[3] It will be evident that the approach of Mr. Richards' book is markedly different from the one I have adopted. My intention, as already indicated, is to show Coleridge's critical ideas in relation to the philosophy from which they were derived and the philosophy which they preceded. Mr. Richards' object is to interpret an idealistic critic by materialistic categories: "I write then as a Materialist trying to interpret before you the utterances of an extreme Idealist" (*Coleridge on Imagination*, p. 19). His materialistic approach is consistently carried out. In speaking of Coleridge's "postulate of philosophy," "Know thyself," Mr. Richards writes, "The rest of his philosophy is a verbal machine for exhibiting what the exercise of this postulate yielded" (*ibid.*, p. 47). Perhaps the best example of what a nonidealistic approach will produce is to be found in the excellent chapter entitled "The Boundaries of the Mythical," in which idealistic metaphysics is treated as a useful (in the best sense of that word) mythology. Cf. esp. pp. 180, 181.

more frequent practice of treating the two fields separately, although it has some justification from the chaotic and unfinished state of Coleridge's writings, is still subject to correction. For a person who finds the definition of imagination hopelessly vague I have the greatest sympathy; yet I believe that there is embodied in that definition a principle which had rich, if somewhat incoherent, results.

When we consider Coleridge's philosophy, we see that it depends for content upon a systematic activity at work in both man and nature, finding its highest expression by man in works of art. The artistic imagination grasps the method of this activity and so comes to grips with reality. It is, of course, unnecessary for the artist to recognize the dialectic of this philosophy consciously; the mere possession of higher imagination will enable him intuitively to feel and artistically to express the structure of the world. For Coleridge believed that he had here an adequate description of the universe, one which revealed its true nature. If this were so, then it would follow that a great artist, a Shakespeare or Milton, who brushes aside the inscrutability of things for a moment and reaches their reality, would do so in accordance with the system described by this philosophy. In one sense, art and philosophy are both trying to discover what is most real. But they differ in approach. The philosopher rationalizes from a basic assumption or root metaphor; the artist depends upon emotional and imaginative as well as intellectual forces. If there is only one reality, the success of either art or philosophy will lie in achieving different versions of the same thing. Implicit in this idea is the relation of philosophical criticism to works of art. The principles explaining the structure of the world which govern the philosophy are found to be valid also for the work of art; they serve to explain, illuminate, and evaluate. The element of evaluation is important because it involves the acceptance of a standard; that is, the value of the work of art is determined by the degree of its congruity with the philosophical system.

In Coleridge, that standard is set by the systematic activity which forms the main part of his philosophy. I shall now endeavor to explain the activity and the critical use which he made of it. We cannot expect to find in Coleridge a consistent, coherent whole. We expect, rather, to find suggestions rich in potentiality and perhaps faintly tinged with prophecy. In this we shall not be disappointed.

Characteristically, the activity in which he is working is neither fully explained nor rendered entirely consistent within itself. It can, however, be regarded as having two large aspects: the first composed of the system of thesis, antithesis, and synthesis which I have already described, and the second involving a more advanced theory, which I shall call organic unity.[4] The first element is clearly in line with the contemporary German philosophy. Fichte and Schelling admittedly influenced Coleridge in his use of the triad; the debt is certain, and, I believe, very great. But we have already seen that Coleridge found himself dissatisfied with those men, the most obvious reason being their neglect of the living God of Coleridge's faith. However, there may be another reason of more importance to his criticism. It will be remembered that in the *Biographia,* after describing his critical method, he writes:

It will be hereafter my business to construct by a series of intuitions the progressive schemes, that must follow from such a power with such forces, till I arrive at the fulness of the human intelligence. For my present purpose, I assume such a power as my principle, in order to deduce from it a faculty, the generation, agency, and application of which form the contents of the ensuing chapter.[5]

There are two remarks to be made about this passage. First, he was unable to keep his word in the ensuing chapter; his confused account is broken off abruptly, after which there is a bare presentation of the definition of imagination. Second, at no time was he able to construct the series of progressive schemes which he

[4] I am somewhat arbitrarily appropriating this term to designate the unity described by modern objective idealism as opposed to the unity of the triad system developed by Fichte, Schelling, and Hegel.

[5] *B.L.,* Vol. I, p. 188.

mentions. Taken alone, this might be explained as merely another evidence of his inability to pursue a matter to its conclusion; but in the light of passages which reveal the groping of his mind towards a more satisfactory theory, his failure to develop the present one gains in significance.

In spite of the fact that he did not complete his system on the triad basis, he frequently made use, in his literary criticism, of the thesis, antithesis, and synthesis scheme as applied to the synthesis of two given opposites. Alice D. Snyder, in *The Critical Principle of the Reconciliation of Opposites as Employed by Coleridge,* has given many interesting and suggestive examples of this principle at work in his criticism. Perhaps the best example comes in the *Biographia,* where he describes the poet (in reality the function of art):

> This power [i.e., poetic power] ... reveals itself in the balance or reconcilement of opposite or discordant qualities: of sameness with difference; of the general with the concrete; the idea with the image; the individual with the representative; the sense of novelty and freshness with old and familiar objects; a more than usual state of emotion with more than usual order; judgment ever awake and steady self-possession with enthusiasm and feeling profound or vehement; and while it blends and harmonizes the natural and the artificial, still subordinates art to nature; the manner to the matter; and our admiration of the poet to our sympathy with the poetry.[6]

It is interesting to note that this paragraph comes in the chapter following the one on imagination in which he failed to deduce the definition from his system. It may also be remarked that in this passage he does not strictly follow that system. Here, surely, are opposites in great plenty, although, as Professor Muirhead says,[7] there might have been more. But even if we grant for the moment the oppositeness of his terms (which is by no means certain, as in idea and image, emotion and order), what has become of the carefully ordered, dynamic, and gradually more inclusive scale of triads which was meant to encompass the universe? According to the system at hand, the relation of one pair of oppo-

---

[6] *Ibid.,* Vol. II, p. 12.   [7] *Coleridge as a Philosopher,* p. 209.

sites to another is puzzling. It is difficult to see the relation of "the
general with the concrete" to "sameness with difference," regard-
less of the ease with which we may agree to their presence in a
work of art. It seems an obvious conclusion that they do not fit
and that Coleridge saw no way to make them do so. What he did
see was an artistic principle in which the imagination of the artist blended and fused into a unified whole the many elements
with which he was working. He saw a dynamic quality which
meant life and growth, and which carried the imaginative mind
through the stages of composition until it reached an organic synthesis. I believe the passage quoted above to be peculiarly expres-
sive of Coleridge's state of mind with regard to the philosophy in
which he had been working. He saw there fruitful suggestions
toward a description of the way in which an artist's mind works,
but at the same time he seemed to feel what might be called a
pragmatic dissatisfaction with the scheme as thus evolved. That
is, when it came to a practical application of the system to literature, or aesthetic problems generally, there was a difficulty which
could not be entirely overcome. This difficulty was intrinsic to
the system and perhaps may be described best by the term, formalism. The charge of formalism was brought against idealists
by R. B. Perry. He writes:

> The absolute idealist like the pre-Kantian absolutist necessarily turns to
> those properties of things which have the maximum of generality. Like his
> forerunners, he depends for the definition of his universal principle upon
> the *logical categories. . . .* if consciousness is to be generalized, it must be de-
> fined in logical terms; and when so defined it serves to explain the logical
> elements of experience, *and nothing more. . . .* It is significant that idealism
> loses its pragmatic value, its fruitfulness of application and pertinence to
> life, in proportion to the refinement of its logic.[8]

It follows, then, that one of the difficulties of a system made up of
highly refined, purely logical categories is that when it is applied
to life or literature it is marked by rigidity. In view of the complexity found in the particulars of existence, the terms of the triad

---

[8] *Present Philosophical Tendencies*, pp. 175–176.

become too exacting. For Coleridge, there was little danger of becoming entangled in the attempt to apply rigidly a purely intellectual system of logic to the many-sided presentations of literature. For him, the heart led the way and the head followed. For him, as for the majority of mankind, the purpose of the intellect was to explain, describe, and interpret convictions arrived at emotionally. I have already mentioned his remark, "A metaphysical solution that does not instantly tell you something in the heart is grievously to be suspected as apocryphal."[9] The way Coleridge took to avoid the difficulty of which I have been speaking was characteristic of a man whose principles were held in solution, to be tested and regarded as valuable only so far as they illuminated and explained the life which he saw. As a result, he used in his literary criticism only the elements which agreed with his experience. Those elements were two: the dynamic activity in literature, and the power of the imagination to blend or fuse opposite or discordant qualities. Observe that in the quotation cited above he did not insist upon the exact oppositeness of the qualities; he also included those which were merely discordant. In doing so, he diverged from the triad scheme.

Because of this only partial agreement of his philosophy as stated with his literary criticism, attempts to demonstrate the relation of the two have not met with full success. It is my belief that the greater part of his criticism is more truly based on a theory which did not take definite philosophical shape until late in the nineteenth century under the hands, first, of T. H. Green, and later, of F. H. Bradley and Bernard Bosanquet. Although it is true that Coleridge never worked out the theory in detail, nevertheless, evidence of its presence in his mind both in aesthetic theorizing and in literary criticism is striking. This theory, which may be called the organic unity of objective idealism, resembles in many ways the triad system; but it varies importantly in that it escapes the rigidity inherent in the latter scheme and becomes

---

[9] *Letters*, p. 428. See above, pp. 5 and 13. For another expression of the idea, see Raysor, *op. cit.*, Vol. II, pp. 286–287.

a more flexible and adaptable instrument. It may be used to describe the work of art in a more illuminating way because it agrees more closely with human experience.

A brief review of the modern idea of organic unity will be helpful in describing the way in which Coleridge's mind caught certain fundamentals of that system without being able to make the advance on contemporaneous philosophy which came later in the century. As exemplified by Bosanquet, modern idealism begins with the same assertions of the priority of cognitive consciousness and of a dynamic active force at work in both man and nature that was characteristic of the earlier kind. Bosanquet writes, speaking of the ideal, ". . . it means the heightened expression of character and individuality which come of a faith *in the life and divinity with which the external world is instinct and inspired*."[10] These assertions in one form or another are held by modern idealists universally. The element which particularly distinguishes them from the Schelling and Hegel sort is the treatment they make of the form which this dynamic activity takes. We have already seen that the German philosophers of the early nineteenth century evolved the triad. From that formula there was developed the modern system which may be designated as organic unity, organic form, or coherence. Generally speaking, this system has four characteristics, which may be listed[11] as follows:

1. It is an organizing process, growing in richness. Given any single appearance, other appearances will be attracted to it which fuse or blend and thus become organized. The additional appearances add complexity of relationship which means richness.

2. It is a cumulative process. The later stages of any organization include all the relevant appearances of the earlier states as well as the newest additions.

3. It is an economical process. All relevant appearances are saved; only those irrelevant are thrown away. But there are no

---

[10] *Three Lectures on Aesthetic*, p. 63.

[11] I am following the formulation of the characteristics of organic unity made by Professor S. C. Pepper, of the University of California.

appearances which are not relevant to something; each one finds its place in its proper organization.

4. It is a spontaneous process. It is inevitable and happens of its own accord. The scientist or artist who organizes material is a mere agent. This is the result of the conception of a dynamic active force at work in both man and nature, and has as a corollary the theory that in any single stage there is the potentiality and, in a sense, the prophecy of all later stages.

This process is a description of the way life works, and therefore is subject to universal application. It may be seen in the development of any science, in the growth of a body of knowledge, in the structure of a play, a poem, a statue, in the developing personality of a human being. Any phenomenon or appearance finds its appropriate place within an organization.

Coleridge once wrote: "To trace the if not absolute birth, yet growth and endurance of language, from the mother talking to the child at her breast. O what a subject for some happy moment of deep feeling and strong imagination."[12] Had he ever done this, we would have a perfect example of the process I have been describing. It will be interesting to indicate superficially the stages of such a growth, taking at the same time a side glance at the artist working upon his material, and indicate, in both, the functioning of organic unity.

The first stage of language in a child consists of isolated words, such as "mama," "daddy," "kitty." At the earliest stage, however, these words are not specific in their meaning; thus, "kitty" may mean not only a cat, but any animal. There is in this stage the minimum of structure and so the minimum of meaning. This stage is paralleled by the stage in the artistic process when a writer first comes upon "material" for him to work upon. His material is vague, unrelated: it may mean any of a number of things when it becomes more structural. The next stage in the development of language in a child is when the denotation of his words becomes specific. When this happens, when, for instance, "kitty" means

---

[12] *A.P.*, p. 95.

nothing but "cat," the organizing process begins and the child learns to combine nouns and verbs, making such simple sentences as "Kitty runs." The writer at this stage perceives certain fundamental relationships, such as, for instance, the relationship of a character's motives to his actions—a relationship which may be modified because of the interaction of other influences later, but which will remain essentially the same. For both the child and the writer this process involves new relationships, which means that there is greater significance because of a more complex, richer organization. It may be observed here that complexity, meaning number and degree of organization of appearances, is synonymous with richness. Gradually the organization grows. For the child there is the apprehension of phrases, clauses, and other grammatical elements. There is also his constantly more knowing use of speech rhythms, his perception of the place played in language by slang, colloquialisms, and idiom. All these things are being located in that structure which is language.

The growth of this knowledge is cumulative. When the child is in grammar school and is able to write simple compositions, his ability is the result of all his former experience in language, beginning with the isolated words of his earliest speech and ending with the last lesson in grammar which has added new relations. All previous relevant stages are present; the simple sentence, the complex, the pronoun reference, the idiomatic use of the preposition. The result of these additions is cumulative: each element or "appearance" stands in a slightly different and firmer relationship to the whole than it did before. The process through which a writer goes exhibits the same characteristic. All that he has done before is present, informing and giving structure to what he is trying to shape at the moment.

This growth is economical in the sense that all relevant appearances are saved and become part of it. Each word, each relation, the significance added by the correction of error, finds its place in the organization. But in the growth of any structure many appearances will be encountered which seem to be relevant but are not. The first inarticulate cries of the child are discarded as language. Childish words are discarded along with unidiomatic slang. For the writer, any correction on a manuscript may mean that an irrelevant appearance has been excluded.

According to this theory, the process is spontaneous, that is, the appearances organize themselves. The child who makes the connection between a noun and a verb, the writer at work on a poem, is acting merely as an agent. Of the four characteristics, this is perhaps the hardest for nonidealistic common sense to accept. The child does not create the connections, he discovers them. The artist, in spite of his labor, writes the poem by necessity. This view will serve to explain the many claims of inspiration by poets; the names of Milton, Yeats, and Coleridge himself at once come to mind. But for evidence of the common-sense sort, there is no need to rely upon the examples offered by geniuses. The experience of watching a manuscript, no matter how prosaic, grow under your own hand will illustrate the principle. The material itself seems to demand a certain sort of structure, to be apart from and external to your personal desires or prejudices.

The process I have been describing *is* organic unity. It is what an idealist means when he speaks of form. Let us now turn to Bosanquet's discussion of form. He writes that form and substance are really one in principle, but that by a logical fiction we continue to contrast them because "there is always some failure to bring them quite together." The correctness of applying any such term as "form" to my experience "depends on the degree of insight with which the object of experience is appreciated, and of course, on the degree of life and structure which a thing actually possesses."[12] Defining form, he writes:

So (i) form means outline, shape, general rule, e.g. for putting together a sentence or an argument; or it means the metre in poetry, or the type of poem, sonnet or what not. In all these it is something superficial, general, diagrammatic. We speak of empty form, mere form, formal politeness; it is opposed to the heart and soul of anything, to what is essential, material, and so forth.

[12] Bosanquet, *op. cit.*, p. 13.

But (ii) when you push home your insight into the order and connection of parts, not leaving out the way in which this affects the parts themselves; then you find that the form becomes (as a lawyer would say) "very material"; not merely outlines and shapes, but all the acts of gradations and variations and connections that make anything what it is—the life, soul, and movement of the object.[14]

This conception of form leads directly to the idealistic theory of imagination. Bosanquet writes, "The imagination is precisely the mind at work, pursuing and exploring the possibilities suggested by the connections of its experience."[15] It is "active and creative. . . . The mind is freely reconstructing and remodeling all that perception presents to it in the direction which promises the maximum of form."[16]

A child learning a language is "pushing home his insight into the order and connection of parts." If he is imaginative, the possibilities of exploring connections and relations will be increased enormously and his experience in language proportionately enriched.

---

[14] Bosanquet, *op. cit.*, p. 13.

[15] *Ibid.*, p. 26.

[16] *Ibid.*

V. ORGANIC UNITY IN NATURE
AND IN LITERATURE

THE MODERN THEORY makes its presence felt not only in Coleridge's aesthetics, but in his discussions of nature as well. Perhaps the best evidence of later objective idealism in his nonliterary writings is to be found in a manuscript, as yet unpublished, in the possession of the Rev. Gerard H. B. Coleridge, of Leatherhead. The extract I am about to quote has been printed by Professor J. H. Muirhead:

The true object of Natural Philosophy is to discover a central Phenomenon in Nature, and a central Phenomenon requires and supposes a central thought in Mind. The *Notional* Boundaries or Ne plus ultras of Nature are a part that relatively to no minor particles is a whole, i.e. an Atom: and a Whole, which in no relation is a Part, i.e. a Universe. ... Not the imagination alone, but the Reason requires a Centre. It is a necessary postulate of Science. That therefore which can be found nowhere absolutely and exclusively must be imagined everywhere relatively and partially. Hence the law of Bicentrality, i.e. that every Whole, whether without parts or composed of parts, and, in the former whether without parts by defect or lowness of Nature (= a material atom), or without parts by the excellence of its Nature (= a Monad or Spirit) must be conceived as a possible centre in itself, and at the same time as having a centre out of itself and common to it with all other parts of the same System. Now the first and fundamental Postulate of Universal Physiology, comprising both organic and inorganic Nature—or—the fundamental position of the *Philosophy* of Physics and Physiology—is: that there is in Nature a tendency to realize this possibility wherever the conditions exist: and the first problem of this Branch of Science, is, What are the conditions under which a Unit having a centre in the distance can manifest its own centrality, i.e. be the centre of a system and (as, in dynamics, the power of the centre acts in every point of the area contained in the circumference) be the centre and the copula ... of a system. Such a unit would have three characters:

1. It would be a component part of a system, having a centre out of itself, or to use a geometrical metaphor, it would be a point in some one of the concentrical lines composing a common circle.

2. It would be itself the centre and copula, the attractive and cohesive force, of a system of its own.

3. *For itself* (as far as it exists for itself) it would be the centre of the universe in a perpetual tendency to include whatever else exists relatively to it in itself, and what it could not include, to repel. Whatever is not contained in the System, of which it is the centre and copula, either does not exist at all *for* it or exist as an alien, which it resists, and in resisting either appropriates (digestion, assimilation), or repels, or ceases to be, i.e. dies.[1]

Coleridge now remarks that the philosopher may regard any body in reference to a common center, the action of which center constitutes the general laws of the system; but in this view all bodies are contemplated as inanimate, and the aggregate of inanimate bodies is called inorganic nature. He continues:

Or, he may contemplate a body as containing its centre or principle of Unity in itself; and, as soon as he ascertains the existence of the conditions requisite to the manifestations of such a principle, he supposes Life and these bodies collectively are named Organic Nature. In Nature there is a tendency to respect herself so as to attempt in each part what she had produced in the Whole, but with a limited power and under certain conditions. N.B. In this, the only scientific view, Nature itself is assumed as the Universal principle of life, and like all other Powers, is contemplated under the two primary Ideas of Identity and Multeity, i.e. alternately as one and as many. In other words, exclusively of *degree* as subsisting in a series of different intensities.

There is in this long quotation a remarkable similarity to the ideas expressed by the system of objective idealism or organic unity as I have described it.[2] Coleridge's statement of the law of bicentrality by which any whole (for "whole" we may substitute unit, appearance, or phenomenon) must be conceived as a possible outcome in itself and at the same time as having a center out of itself and common to it with all other parts of the same system, is thoroughly in accord with modern theory.

The language of a child, for example, has an individual growth with its own dynamic center, but it also has its proper place in the total organization of the universe. To use Coleridge's figure, it

[1] *Op. cit.*, pp. 122 ff.

[2] Bosanquet uses the same illustration of circle and center to describe his theory (*Principle of Individuality and Value*, p. 39). For a looser expression of the same idea in Coleridge, see *A.P.*, p. 298.

would be a point in one of the concentrical lines composing a circle. The complete circle with all its concentric lines represents the universe. The principle of individual growth furthers the similarity between Coleridge and the moderns. *For itself,* the language of a child would be the center of the universe, having a perpetual tendency to include all that is relevant to it. The growth reaches out and gathers in as many relations as may affect it. Each one of these relations then becomes a part of the organization. Appearances which are not part of the system are drawn in and become part of it if relevant, or if irrelevant are repelled and find their place in a different organization. In the same way that the moderns conceive of any given appearance as having its principle of unity within itself, so does Coleridge, who says that if a body be so considered, then as soon as the philosopher ascertains what conditions are necessary to the manifestation of such a principle, he supposes that life and these bodies collectively are named organic nature.

This idea of unity receives further elaboration in the essay, "Theory of Life."[3] Here life is defined as the principle of individuation, a principle which is in no way to be distinguished from the theory of nature I have been discussing. Life, as organization from within, is opposed to mechanism, which is organization from without, or form forced upon material. Life is found to be a property of matter in all its forms, of which man is the highest. He writes:

> In the lowest forms of the vegetable and animal world, we perceive totality dawning into individuation, while in man, as the highest class, the individuality is not only perfected in its corporeal sense, but begins a new series beyond the appropriate limits of physiology. The tendency to individuation, more or less obvious, constitutes the common character of all classes, so far as they maintain for themselves a distinction from the universal life of the planet; while the degrees, both of intensity and extension, to which this tendency is realized, form the species and their ranks in the great scale of ascent and expansion.[4]

[3] Written by Coleridge in collaboration with Gilman, but thoroughly representative of Coleridge in thought.

[4] "Theory of Life," *Miscellanies, Aesthetic and Literary*, p. 390.

By "totality dawning into individuation" Coleridge seems to indicate that "whole," "unit," or "appearance" from which organic growth begins. It is totality only in his special sense of the word, which means not totality as it is commonly understood, but that single element which starts a growth towards totality. As the growth progresses and becomes more complex in adding new relationships, it has more individuation or, to use the familiar word, individuality. The point in this discussion which is important for his aesthetics lies in the conception of individuality. To the common-sense view, individuality frequently means that which is unique or peculiar to one person; its essence lies in something strong in itself and sharply detached from life around it. Individualism or individuality is often directly opposed to universality or catholicity. This is not true of Coleridge, who looks upon individuality as something strong in itself, to be sure, but more particularly as a force which reaches out and makes new connections and relations. The greatest individuality is that which has the greatest degree of organization, the largest quantity of relations.[5]

In the foregoing pages we have seen in Coleridge a nonliterary statement of organic unity which bears a remarkably close resemblance to the modern theory of organic unity as exemplified by Bernard Bosanquet. I have already remarked, and I wish now to reaffirm, that Coleridge's ideas on this subject were never elaborated into a complete system. They are, however, present in his critical writings in such great force as to render an attempt to explain his criticism by the triad system difficult and on the whole inadequate. It is undeniably true that the synthesis of antitheses was frequently present in his mind when he was explaining an aesthetic theory or criticizing an actual work of art; it is equally true, however, that the later theory was also there, modifying the

---

[5] In a comment on Shakespeare, Coleridge gives an excellent example of individuality: "Shakespeare had virtually surveyed all the great component powers and impulses of human nature, seen that the different combinations and subordinations were the <great> *individualizers* of men and showed their harmony by the effects of disproportion either of excess or deficiency" (Raysor, *op. cit.,* Vol. I, p. 233).

rigidity of the opposites, questioning the exactness of their opposition, and enriching the significance of that dynamic progression which the earlier and later theories have in common.

I turn now to the idea of organic unity as it appears in Coleridge's aesthetic and critical writings. Perhaps the clearest explanations occur when he makes a distinction between mechanical
and organic form:

> The form is mechanic, when on any given material we impress a pre-
> determined form, not necessarily arising out of the properties of the ma-
> terial;—as when to a mass of wet clay we give whatever shape we wish it
> to retain when hardened. The organic form on the other hand, is innate;
> it shapes, as it develops itself from within, and the fulness of its develop-
> ment is one and the same with the perfection of its outward form. Such
> is the life, such the form. Nature, the prime genial artist, inexhaustible in
> divers powers, is equally inexhaustible in forms. Each exterior is the physi-
> ognomy of the being within, its true image reflected and thrown out from
> the concave mirror. And even such is the appropriate excellence of her
> chosen poet, of our own Shakespeare. . . .[6]

Organic form, as thus explained, agrees pretty closely with the
modern theory. Coleridge says it is innate; that is, it is within
the material originally. Mechanical form, on the other hand, is
always an arbitrary stamp or mold impressed from without.
That which is organic "shapes, as it develops, itself from within";
that is, it is a spontaneous, dynamic progression. The artist who
organizes the material is a mere agent. "The fulness of its development is one and the same with the perfection of its outward
form." By this, Coleridge means that when a work of art having
organic unity, such as *Hamlet* or *Lear,* is finished, a cumulative
process will have taken place; so that a spectator will not only
feel, in the fullness of the action's development, the force of all
that has gone before, but will also feel that the play was destined
by its own nature to last exactly five acts and to come to the conclusion which Shakespeare gave it. When this occurs, the distinction made by an ordinary mind between content and form breaks
down because the content has the form within it and in this sense

---

[6] Raysor, *op. cit.,* Vol. I, p. 224.

constitutes the form. This is indicated by Coleridge in the line, "Such is the life, such the form." The quotation from Bosanquet, given before, contains approximately the same idea when he says that the form is "all the acts of gradations and variations and connections that make anything what it is—the life, soul, and movement of the object." Coleridge goes on, then, to pay Shakespeare the highest compliment in his power, by drawing a comparison between nature and him. Just as the outer forms of nature are certain reflections of the spirit within and therefore have organic unity, according to Coleridge's metaphysics, so the outer forms of Shakespeare's creations, because of his imaginative insight into the process of nature, reflect inevitably the true core of his work. Only by means of the secondary or higher imagination, which "dissolves, diffuses, dissipates, in order to re-create" and in so doing reveals the true structure of the universe, is Shakespeare able to create works of art having organic unity.[7]

Mechanical form or unity, on the other hand, is the result of superimposing upon material a predetermined form, not necessarily arising out of the properties of the material. It is always the creation of man and so is artificial in that it is never found in nature. The person who creates mechanical form is the possessor of primary imagination (since all mankind has this) and of fancy, but not of secondary imagination. Such a person can play only with that which is fixed and definite; his faculty is that of mere memory, emancipated from the order of time and space, by means of which he is enabled arbitrarily to rearrange the material which is his. Thus there is the same connection between mechanical form and fancy that there is between organic form and secondary imagination.

Coleridge illustrates the distinction between mechanical and organic form with a comparison between the work of Shake-

---

[7] On another occasion, Coleridge made the distinction with regard to art in general: "Remember that there is a difference between form as proceeding and shape as super-induced;—the latter is either the death or imprisonment of the thing;—the former is its self-witnessing and self-effected sphere of agency" (*B.L.*, Vol. I, p. 262). See also Raysor, *op. cit.*, Vol. I, p. 5.

speare and that of Beaumont and Fletcher considered as one artist. Take the first scene of *Bonduca,* he says, and compare it with
any scene from *Richard II* which is of about the same length and
which consists mostly of long speeches. He continues:

> That of B. and F. you will find a well arranged bed of flowers, each having
> its separate root, and its position determined aforehand by the will of the
> gardener,—each fresh plant a fresh volition. In the former [Shakespeare]
> you see an Indian fig tree as described by Milton;—all is growth, evolu-
> tion; ... each line, each word almost, begets the following, and the will
> of the writer is an interfusion, a continuous agency, and not a series of sep-
> arate acts. Shakespeare is the height, breadth and depth of Genius: Beau-
> mont and Fletcher the excellent mechanism, in juxta-position and succes-
> sion, of talent.[8]

The distinction shows the difference between a living and an
artificial product. In Shakespeare there is a dynamic progression
which, evolving, has organic unity. In Beaumont and Fletcher
there is a series of units which are never welded together. Coleridge by no means finds Beaumont and Fletcher valueless; he
merely makes the point that their work differs from Shakespeare's in kind rather than in degree, that *Bonduca* has the mer-
its of an excellent mechanism but lacks the virtue of a work which
is alive. Shakespeare's kind is, of course, infinitely higher.[9]

The distinction of which I have been speaking was later ampli-
fied by Coleridge when he asserted that Shakespeare, following
the law of nature, *could* not produce a work which had mechanical form:

> What had a grammatical and logical consistency for the ear,—what could
> be put together and represented to the eye,—these poets [Beaumont and
> Fletcher] took from the ear and eye, unchecked by any intuition of an

---

[8] *Works,* 1847 ed., Vol. XIV, p. 317.

[9] There can be no doubt that Coleridge *on idealistic grounds* attached at all times a
higher value to imagination than to fancy. Works produced by imagination embody concretely the real structure of a good universe; works produced by fancy do not. But if
idealistic grounds are given up and materialistic, as in Mr. I. A. Richards' *Coleridge on
Imagination,* are substituted, there is merely a probable, not a necessary, higher value in
imagination. Mr. Richards' account is an interesting example of the different results
which a materialistic approach to Coleridge will produce. Cf. *Coleridge on Imagination,*
pp. 91, 92.

inward impossibility;—just as a man might put together a quarter of an orange, a quarter of an apple, and the like of a lemon and a pomegranate, and make it look like a round diverse-coloured fruit. But nature which works from within by evolution according to a law, cannot do so, nor could Shakespeare; for he too worked in the spirit of nature, by evolving the germ from within by the imaginative power according to an idea. For as the power of seeing is to light, so is an idea in mind to a law in nature. They are correlatives, which suppose each other.[10]

This is an extremely valuable passage, because it places Coleridge in accord with later idealists who look upon the artist as a mere agent in whose mind the appearances organize themselves spontaneously. If a man has an imagination which enables him to perceive, see, or feel the law in nature, his mind will *by necessity* organize in accordance with that law the work of art which he is creating. To paraphrase Coleridge's simile: just as a man who has the power of vision is forced to see light, so is a man who has imaginative insight into a law of nature forced to organize his material in accordance with that law. Beaumont and Fletcher lacked such insight and so, when they wrote a play, were "unchecked by any intuition of an inward impossibility." The last two words are accurate, because a product of mechanical organization is impossible, according to Coleridge, in the sense that it is unreal. A fruit made by putting quarters of four different fruits together may have an existence in time and space; but it can never have reality, because it lacks the essential core and growth which there is in nature, and which is called organic unity. Coleridge again emphasizes the most important element by saying that "in the Shakespearian drama there is a vitality which grows and evolves itself from within,—a keynote which guides and controls the harmonies throughout." He continues: "What is *Lear?* It is storm and tempest—the thunder at first grumbling in the far horizon, then gathering around us, and at length bursting in fury over our heads,—succeeded by a breaking of the clouds for a while, a last flash of lightning, the closing in of night, and the single hope of darkness."[11] In other words, the

---

[10] *Works*, 1847 ed., Vol. XIV, p. 43.   [11] *Ibid.*, p. 44.

succession of storm and sunlight in nature is an expression of the same unity which there is in *Lear*. So much for the philosophical side of the metaphor; but it took a man who was a poet as well as a philosopher to write that last phrase, "the single hope of darkness," which so powerfully expresses the strength of pity and fear compacted in the end of the play. *Macbeth,* too, has a "keynote which guides and controls the harmonies throughout." It is "deep and earthy,—composed to the subterranean music of a troubled conscience which converts everything into the wild and fearful."[12]

Although mechanical and organic unity differ in kind, it is still possible that parts of a work may be "in correspondence with nature" and therefore organic in those parts, yet lack the higher unity as a whole. This circumstance is true of Beaumont and Fletcher, but there is no danger of anyone's being misled, because, ". . . the false source is always discoverable, first by the gross contradictions to nature in so many other parts, and secondly, by the want of the impression which Shakespeare makes, that the thing said not only might have been said, but that nothing else could be substituted, so as to excite the same sense of its exquisite propriety."[13] It is significant to observe that in the second reason given by Coleridge, the feeling for the right word, there lies a philosophical explanation of one of the most universally used and at the same time baffling principles of practical criticism. When Matthew Arnold adopted this principle in his "touchstone" theory, he was able to say no more, in effect, than: "Here is poetry which is intrinsically great. Read it and listen to it and you will understand its greatness." Coleridge is able to give a richer understanding of the same principle because his explanation is the result of closer thinking.

Coleridge goes on to consider, with reference to the source of an author's material, the relation of the author to the characters whom he creates. Shakespeare shaped his characters out of the nature within; but it is not safe to say that he did so out of his

---

[12] *Ibid.*   [13] *Ibid.*

own nature as an individual person, because the latter is a mere effect or product, not a power. Coleridge explains:

> It was Shakespeare's prerogative to have the universal, which is potentially in each particular, opened out to him, the homo generalis, not as an abstraction from observation of a variety of men, but as the substance capable of endless modifications, of which his own personal existence was but one, and to use this one as the eye that beheld the other, and as the tongue that could convey the discovery.[14]

Shakespeare, then, through his imaginative power was enabled to see the universal in the particular, and, unlike the great majority of artists, to look upon his own personal existence as merely one of a multitude of particulars. The potentiality in the particular strikes the heart of modern idealism. Any given appearance or particular contains within itself the potentiality of the universal. The particular gains individuality as it grows, and the whole process from the particular to the universal is what is meant by organic unity. It is important to note that Shakespeare's power does not come from a synthesis of his observations of particular men—that would be mere fancy working by means of memory—, but from the power of endlessly modifying a given particular. The modifying process is that which expands, opens out, evolves; and it has as its root a single idea or appearance.

The dramatist who does not have this power of seeing the universal in the particular is forced to fall back upon his own personal experience, and in so doing reveals his lack of imaginative insight. Moreover, since the very great artists are necessarily few in number, this fault of drawing out of themselves is one of the most common vices of dramatic writers. As a result: "In Beaumont and Fletcher you have descriptions of characters by the poet rather than the characters themselves; we are told, and impressively told, of their being; but we rarely or never feel that they actually are."[15] Again philosophical theory evolves a highly practical criticism. The reality of the characters must be one of the basic tests of the worth of a play; yet a criticism which attempts

---

[14] *Works*, 1847 ed., Vol. XIV, p. 45.   [15] *Ibid*.

to define such a reality, but which lacks a guiding principle, very frequently deteriorates into mere impressionism. Under Coleridge's criticism, the unreality of the characters of Beaumont and Fletcher lies in the fact that they are the result of a description drawn from the author's experience, rather than the result of a creation evolved through imaginative power.

In one sense, this distinction between sources of an author's material is a distinction between dramatic and lyric. Coleridge says, "Beaumont and Fletcher are the most lyrical of our dramatists."[18] In the sense that drawing out of and giving expression to your own experience is the quality which makes a work lyrical, such a distinction is correct. However, I do not believe Coleridge meant to assert that because a work was lyrical it could not have organic unity nor be the result of higher imagination. Although he does not make the point clear, the position he takes does not necessitate such an assertion. It would be consistent with his theory to say that a lyric has organic unity when the author takes his own personal experience, which is in no way to be differentiated from particulars external to himself, and brings to bear upon it the power of higher imagination. In his discussion of drama, however, Coleridge is interested chiefly in character and action, and so does not develop his statement that Beaumont and Fletcher are the "most lyrical of our dramatists."

The distinction already made, that Shakespeare creates his characters and so differs from lesser artists, who merely describe theirs, is elaborated in a discussion of Massinger's satire. In Massinger the satire is weakened because the characters satirized have no reality; the observer feels that Massinger has arbitrarily attributed a quality to his character and then satirized him for possessing it. In the *Maid of Honor* the Sylli "come forward to declare themselves fools ad arbitrium auctoris, and so the diction always needs the subintelligitur ('the man looks as if he thought so and so,') expressed in the language of the satirist and not in that of the man himself. . . . The author mixes his own feelings and judg-

---
[18] *Ibid.*

ments concerning the presumed fool."[17] The man himself fights, as it were, against the judgment of the author and shows that he is no fool at all, but rather a man of wit making merry with himself. Such a result nullifies the satire and prevents the author from realizing his intention. In Shakespeare, on the contrary, the characters "evolved themselves according to their incidental proportions, from excess, deficiency etc."[18] Because they are real, the satire is effective and functions as a truthful criticism of the thing satirized. In other words, the satire upon a character who is created and thus made to live, as in Shakespeare, is not only more effective, but is different from and higher in kind than the satire upon a character who is merely described. This difference is simply another illustration of the distinction between organic and mechanical form.

In general there is a want of preparation in the decisive acts of Massinger's characters because, like Beaumont and Fletcher, he plans each one separately and fails to conceive properly the relation of the individual character to the play as a whole.[19] This failure to think in terms of organic unity results in the author's interfering with his characters in two ways: First, he may take a dislike to them and spite himself upon them "by making them talk like fools or monsters, as Fulgentio in his visit to Camiola" (*Maid of Honor,* Act II, sc. 2). Second, he may intrude his personal and therefore petty grievances upon the play by "continued flings at kings, courtiers, and all the favourites of fortune, like one who has intellect enough to see injustice in his own inferiority in the share of the good things of life, but not genius enough to rise above it, and forget himself."[20] Either of these two circumstances is distinctly a fault because the result is a combination of the author with his play rather than the play standing by itself in the unity of its conception.

In spite of these drawbacks, Massinger is a very considerable artist. He often rises into the truly tragic and pathetic, and he excels in narration. We may say that fragments of his plays achieve

---

[17] *Works,* 1847 ed., Vol. XIV, p. 49.   [18] *Ibid.*   [19] *Ibid.*   [20] *Ibid.,* p. 50.

greatness, but that they remain fragments, unrelated organically to the whole of which they are a part. Coleridge compares him to a Flemish painter, "in whose delineations objects appear as they do in nature, have the same force and truth, and produce the same effect upon the spectator."[21] So far, so good; but it is not nearly far enough, for the objects remain isolated.

In contrasting Massinger with Shakespeare, Coleridge has two illuminating explanations, philosophical in nature, yet successful, because of the closeness of their application, in entering the realm of practical criticism. The first explanation corresponds exactly to the passage quoted before, where he explains that a unit in nature has, first, a center out of itself, that it is a component part of a larger system; and second, a center in itself, that it is the center of a system of its own. So it is in Shakespeare: the play represents the whole; each character represents the unit of nature which has its own center but is at the same time a member of a larger organization. Coleridge writes: ". . . in Shakespeare, the play is syngensia; each character has, indeed, a life of its own, and is an individuum of itself, but yet an organ of the whole, as the heart in the human body."[22] The illustration of the circle in which the large enclosure represents the total unity and one of the concentric lines represents the unity of one of the component elements is applicable equally to the unity of nature and to the unity of a play. The critic who is merely practical may react to disharmony in a play as surely as did Coleridge; yet, because of his lack of well-grounded principles, he is confined to a statement and description of it which seems to depend upon a merely personal reaction.

The second explanation of the art of Shakespeare as contrasted to Massinger's pertains to the richness of human experience which almost all critics have found in his plays. Again there is a very close correspondence between his previously quoted philosophical theory and his literary criticism. According to Coleridge, any given unit in nature has a perpetual tendency to include

---

[21] *Ibid.*, p. 51.   [22] *Ibid.*, p. 49.

whatever else exists relatively to it in itself. The number of relationships included in any system is a certain sign of the system's value. In Shakespeare there is found an extraordinary richness and complexity of relationships involved in whatever he is considering: "Shakespeare always by metaphors and figures involves in the thing considered a universe of past and possible experiences; he mingles earth, sea, and air, gives a soul to everything, and at the same time that he inspires human feelings, adds a dignity in his images to human nature itself."[23] It is important to remember that these "metaphors and figures" are not mere decorations or elaborations, but are real and vital elements of the work, and that by reason of their presence the play is enabled to express, not only its own center with more truth and beauty, but also the relation it bears to that totality which is the universe.

As an illustration of the passage cited above, Coleridge quotes the Shakespearean sonnet which begins, "Full many a glorious morning have I seen," and concludes his discussion with the quotation, feeling no doubt, that the richness he has been speaking of must be clear, in that sonnet, to every listener.

Coleridge throws further light on his conception of organic unity in the brief passages in which he discusses the modern novel. In the modern novel, "there is no imagination, but a miserable struggle to excite and gratify mere curiosity.... [the novels] afford excitement without producing reaction."[24] By reaction, he means "an activity of the intellectual faculties, which shows itself in consequent reasoning and observation, and originates action and conduct according to a principle."[25] This activity may be looked upon as "internal causality or the energy of the will on the mind itself."[26] Such an internal causality may be briefly expressed by the word "imagination."[27] Coleridge is writing here, of course, with reference to the effect upon the reader. The lack of reaction produced by a novel does not seem to be in any way intrinsic to the type as literature, but merely happens to be characteristic of the novels, particularly the "fashionable lady's" novels,

---

[23] *Works,* 1847 ed., Vol. XIV, p. 51.   [24] *Ibid.,* p. 143.   [25] *Ibid.*   [26] *Ibid.*   [27] *Ibid.*

with which Coleridge happens to be familiar. The result, then, of a novel is merely to excite and gratify curiosity. A novel is interesting, but lacks harmony and growth. So far as thought is concerned, it may be considered as "external causality in which the train of thought may be considered as the result of outward impressions . . . of fancy, or the associations of memory."[28] Thus we have the old opposition of fancy and imagination. If a novel possessed organic unity it would have that internal causality which stimulates the imagination; because it lacks that unity, in being merely interesting, it has external causality, which means no more than an appeal to the fancy.

The foregoing discussion is further illustrated in a letter of Crabbe Robinson's which describes a lecture given by Coleridge in May, 1808. According to the letter, Coleridge told of being asked by an "amiable lady" in what way Richardson was inferior to Shakespeare. The reply was that Richardson "evinces an exquisite perception of minute feeling, but there is a want of harmony, a vulgarity in his sentiment; he is *only* interesting."[29] Speaking of Richardson's immorality, he says: "The lower passions of our nature are kept through seven or eight volumes, in a hot-bed of interest. Fielding is far less pernicious, for the gusts of laughter drive away sensuality."[30] Coleridge did not share the view, held by Dr. Johnson among many others, that Richardson was both a better artist and a better moralist then Fielding. Coleridge's chief criticism of Richardson is the same as his criticism of the novel in general: that he was able to appeal only to small feelings, to cause interest rather than reaction; that his novels lack the evolution and growth which is characteristic of the best art. In general the novel is mechanical rather than organic. This judgment refers, of course, to the novels that had been written rather than to the novel as a theoretical art form. Coleridge does not condemn the form per se.

This discussion involves a general principle which is equally applicable to any form of art. It is interesting to notice that Cole-

---

[28] *Ibid.*   [29] *Ibid.*, p. 333.   [30] *Ibid.*

ridge, who is a much more workable mine of wisdom than many
have thought, has presented an idea which both John Dewey and
I. A. Richards in different ways have developed more fully. The
effect of a work of art is to make a change in the individual, to
alter his emotional and intellectual equipment and so to give him
richer, more satisfying connections with the society in which he
lives. The exact nature of these changes with the complicated and
varying factors which each involves is of course still a matter for
research of the laboratory sort. But at least some of the general
principles seem to be coming to light. It is very characteristic of
Coleridge that he, using his psychological insight in the service
of philosophical criticism, should hit upon an important principle
so early. The difference he is pointing out is the one between a
good detective story and a good novel—between, for example, a
book by Anthony Fielding and one by Virginia Woolf.

   The principle of organic unity, seen from a slightly different
angle, is an integral part of Coleridge's discussion of stage illusion. On the stage there is a combination of fine arts "in an harmonious whole, having a distinct end of its own, to which the
peculiar end of each of the component arts, taken separately, is
made subordinate and subservient, that, namely, of imitating
reality (objects, actions, or passions) under a semblance of reality."[31] He then compares stage illusion to a picture. When an
artist imitates nature the result is meant only as a picture; but
when a forest is presented on the stage it is meant as an actual
forest. It is essential to the picture that we be not deceived into
mistaking it for reality, whereas it is essential to the stage scenery
that we see as much reality in it as its nature permits; for the stage
scenery is not an end in itself, but merely one of the elements
which go into the making of a harmonious whole. Coleridge is
obviously thinking in terms of organic unity here. The "harmonious whole" of the stage presentation is such a unity, but in its
relation to a whole it functions as a part only.

   The result for the audience is that the spectator has "a sort of

[31] Raysor, *op. cit.*, Vol. I, p. 199.

temporary half-faith" which he "encourages in himself and supports by a voluntary contribution on his own part."[32] Coleridge sums it up, saying, "The true stage-illusion in this and in all other things consists—not in the mind's judging it to be a forest, but, in its remission of the judgement that it is not a forest."[33] We are never entirely deluded. A misunderstanding of the question of representation has caused much false criticism: on the one hand by the French, who reason on stage illusion as an actual delusion, and on the other by Dr. Johnson, who, according to Coleridge, denies it altogether in that he "excludes whatever would not be judged probable by us in our coolest state of feeling, with all our faculties in even balance."[34]

In spite of the fact that Coleridge has been talking about the scene presented as a part only, I do not see how the spectator's attitude toward the scenery can be separated from his attitude toward the play as a whole. The creation of stage illusion must finally depend upon the combination of speeches, action, and setting. Although Coleridge does not explicitly shift his ground when talking about the half-faith with which a spectator views a play, he surely shifts it implicitly.

If, then, we assume that the "remission of judgment" applies to the play as a whole, we are able to see in what way the dictum is in accord with Coleridge's general theory. We find him saying, "... the attempt to cause the highest delusion possible to beings in their senses sitting in a theatre is a gross fault, incident only to low minds, which, feeling that they cannot affect the heart or head permanently, endeavor to call forth the momentary affection."[35] In other words, the highest possible delusion calls forth mere excitement—which, when the novel is the excitant, is momentary—rather than reaction, which is "an activity of the intel-

---

[32] *Ibid.,* p. 200.   [33] *Works,* 1847 ed., Vol. XIV, p. 36.

[34] Raysor, *op. cit.,* Vol. I, p. 202. Coleridge is misusing the Doctor here. In the *Preface to Shakespeare,* Johnson stated his position in a way which should bring general agreement: "Imitations produce pain or pleasure, not because they are mistaken for realities, but because they bring realities to mind."

[35] *Works,* 1847 ed., Vol. XIV, p. 36.

lectual faculties, which shows itself in consequent reasoning and observation and originates action according to a principle."[36] If this analysis of the highest delusion is correct, then it is obvious that stage illusion must be explained on other grounds. Coleridge dismisses actual fiction as coming to the same end. The conclusion, then, is that the correct attitude must lie somewhere between these two. A stage presentation is an imitation of life which must maintain a vital connection with life. Only when the spectator keeps this in mind is he able to view a play as a dynamic piece of human experience which becomes organized with his view of the world and adds significance to it. The evolution of this attitude of suspension of disbelief depends upon two things: first, whether the play itself reveals something new and significant,—we might say, whether it has inner consistency of imaginative fusion; second, whether the spectator has the degree of imaginative power necessary to see the intention of the author in the play. If either of these is lacking, the attitude will break down and the play will be mere excitement or nothing. Thus we are led back to the basic principle of organic unity in the work of art and imaginative power in the artist or spectator.

The distinction between mechanical and organic form is further illustrated by Coleridge's attitude toward places which have historical or literary associations. The train of thought aroused by such things is contingent and transitory. He writes:

> I am not certain whether I should have seen with any emotion the mulberry tree of Shakespeare. If it were a tree of no notice in itself, I am sure that I should feel by an effort—with self-reproach at the dimness of the feeling; if a striking tree, I fear that the pleasure would be diminished rather than increased, that I should have no unity of feeling, and find in the constant association of Shakespeare having planted it an intrusion that prevented me wholly (as a whole man) losing myself in the flexures of its branches and intertwining of its roots.[37]

In fewer words, the tree is related to Shakespeare only by association, and mere association is lacking in significance. But Cole-

---

[36] *Works,* 1847 ed., Vol. XIV, p. 36.   [37] *A.P.,* p. 71.

ridge goes farther than an attribution of lack of significance. In his estimation, such associations are positively harmful; for a Shakespeare exists in the mind,

> . . . as pure action, defecated of all that is material and passive. . . . It degrades the sacred feeling, and is to it what stupid superstition is to enthusiastic religion, when a man makes a pilgrimage to see a great man's shin-bone found unmouldered in his coffin. . . . I could be amused by these things, and should be, if there had not been connected with the great name upon which the amusement wholly depends a higher and deeper pleasure, that will not endure the presence of so mean a companion.[88]

In a man whose critical appreciation enables him to see Shakespeare as pure action and thus to rise above the feelings of mere interest and curiosity with which most people regard the tangible reminders of great men, such an assertion is justifiable. But even if we were to express a doubt of the absolute honesty of his assertion, we should still be compelled to admit that his feeling is entirely in accord with his theory. Anything which has organic unity tends to include all relations which are relevant to it, but at the same time it repels all those which are not relevant. So it was with Coleridge. Because his conception of Shakespeare had organic unity, he could not endure the presence of an appearance the relationship of which was merely accidental.

Unquestionably, this conception of unity played a large part in the development of what Saintsbury, who could see no relation between philosophy and criticism, called one of the greatest principles of romantic criticism: that each work must be judged by its appropriateness to the end in view. Each core, or appearance, with which a work of art begins is a separate thing in itself, having a predestined conclusion according to the working of the principle of unity. If we take the form of a Greek drama and impose it as an arbitrary ideal upon an Elizabethan drama, we are doing the latter a great injustice, because the Greek drama arose under different circumstances and had an end in view entirely different from the Elizabethan. This view by no means holds that

[88] *Ibid.*

the classical drama is to be judged by Aristotelian rules and the
modern by the principle we have been discussing; it holds, rather,
that organic unity will be found as surely in Sophocles as in
Shakespeare. Coleridge expresses this by a comparison between
the swan and the dove. We cannot compare their beauties, he says,
by an abstract rule common to both, without reference to the life
and being of the animals themselves. He continues:

... Say rather if, having first seen the dove, we abstracted its outlines, gave
them a false generalization, called them principle or ideal of bird-beauty
and then proceeded to criticize the swan or the eagle;—not less absurd is
it to pass judgement on the works of a poet on the mere ground they have
been called by the same class-name with the works of other poets of other
times and circumstances, or on any ground, indeed save that of their in-
appropriateness to their own end and being, their want of significances, as
symbol and physiognomy.[39]

The same idea is expressed when he says that he was the first to
demonstrate that "the supposed irregularity and extravagances of
Shakespeare were the mere dreams of a pedantry that arraigned
the eagle because it had not the dimensions of a swan."[40]

A critical difficulty similar to the one discussed above lies in
the fact that critics are "enslaved to the habits of their education
and circumstances."[41] Only that which coincides with the peculiarities of their education "appears rational, becoming, or beautiful to them."[42] A true critic must place himself in some central
position "in which he can command the whole; i.e. some general
rule which as founded in reason or faculties common to all men
must therefore apply to all men."[43] The virtue of this lies in the
point that such a critic will not only require something "true in
human nature itself, and independent of all circumstances; but
in the mode of applying it, he will estimate genius and judgment
according to the felicity with which the imperishable soul of intellect shall have adapted itself to the age, the place, and the ex-

[39] Raysor, *op. cit.*, Vol. I, p. 196.   [40] *Ibid.*, p. 126.

[41] *Ibid.*, p. 221. For another expression of this idea see *Table Talk*, 1847 ed., Vol. XX,
p. 295.

[42] Raysor, *op. cit.*, p. 221.   [43] *Ibid.*

isting manners."" The principle by which a true critic estimates a work of art is, of course, organic unity. With such a criterion the fallacy of the historic estimate is impossible. It is interesting to note the similarity between the critic who is enslaved to the habit of his education and circumstances, and the artist who is able to draw only upon his personal experience in creating a work of art. Neither man has the higher imagination, which would enable him to look upon his own life with the same disinterestedness that he has in observing the external world. Just as Massinger imposes his personal prejudices upon a character he has himself created, so do the poorer critics become entangled in the prejudices and peculiarities of their age and thus fail to distinguish that which is permanently and organically beautiful from that which is mechanically organized and transient in significance.

It follows that, given the fundamental principle of unity, a critic should read a work in the spirit of the age for which it was written. If he does not, the subtle relationship of the work to the peculiarities of its age, as set apart from the permanent human values which it possesses, will escape him. Coleridge sums it up: "The man who reads a work meant for immediate effect upon one age with the notions and feelings of another, may be a refined gentleman, but must be a sorry critic."[45]

The passages I have quoted on organic form, defining that form and distinguishing it from the mechanical kind, are the most direct utterances on the subject which Coleridge made in his literary criticism. However, the distinction, going back as it does to imagination and fancy, and having its analogy in reason and understanding, was so central in Coleridge's thought that it became far more than an intellectual theory: it had its full share in his instinctive and emotional attitude toward the world in general. A reflection of this distinction may be seen when he writes that nothing affects him much at the moment it happens. He is either stupefied or indifferent, for a thing at the moment is but a thing

---

" *Ibid.*   [45] *Works,* 1847 ed., Vol. XV, p. 122.

of the moment. To him, it is a mere fragment, lacking in significance because meaning is always derived from a context. Before it can have value for him, "it must be taken up into the mind, diffuse itself through the whole multitude of shapes and thoughts, not one of which it leaves untinged, between [not one of] which and it some new thought is not engendered."[46] In other words, before any incident can have value, it must go through the same harmonious evolution in his mind which he saw at work in the plays of Shakespeare. To Coleridge, impressions in themselves were nothing but the materials out of which a work of art might be made.

There is a passage in the *Anima Poetae* which shows that he was conscious of the fact that the principle of unity he saw in nature and art was present in him subconsciously and furnished the motive for many actions otherwise unexplainable. He tells of sitting before his fire late one night and observing that the blaze had died in such a way that the pieces of smoldering wood resembled the remains of an old edifice. Although he intended to go to bed at that instant, he felt an impulse to put on three pieces of wood that "exactly completed the perishable architecture." Reflecting upon the fact that there could be no possible practical use in doing so, he writes, "Hence I seem (for I write not yet having gone to bed) to suspect that this disease of totalizing and perfecting, may be the bottom impulse of many, many actions, in which it never is brought forward as an avowed or even agnised as a conscious motive."[47] The passage is a striking illustration of movement in form, the incomplete relationships which seemed in themselves to desire a further progress, and felt impelled to complete the structure.

The inclination of poet and philosopher was in him. He recognized this, and, so doing, set himself apart from the ordinary run of human beings; for to him both art and philosophy were subjects for the elect. The higher imagination, the ability to deal with philosophical ideas, was a gift possessed by the few. He illustrates the difference between the poet and philosopher on the one hand and the common man on the other in a way that reveals significantly the manner in which his mind centered on the idea of organic unity. "The first range of hills," he writes, "that encircles the scanty vale of human life, is the horizon for the majority of its inhabitants. On *its* ridges the common sun is born and departs. From *them* the stars rise and touching *them* they vanish."[48] However, in all ages there have been a few who were able to penetrate beyond the first range of hills, to realize something of the high and mysterious sources of the rivers which run through the vale. These men were the poets and philosophers. The metaphor in which Coleridge describes the philosopher (and the poet as well, although he is speaking explicitly only of philosophy here) is in itself an illustration of organic unity. The ordinary man is able to deal only in appearances; his vision is limited to the bare unrelated facts which he sees around him. The first range of hills, taken as a whole, is the core of the growth which, fully developed, would explain the universe. To the philosopher this core begins its growth, reaches out and gathers in new relationships. He sees more than the first range, and even though he may not be able to penetrate to the source of the rivers, to the high and mysterious places (by which Coleridge means God), he is at any rate in a different category from the common man. Here Coleridge is talking about the universe as a whole, but the principle involved is the same as it was when he was talking about the unity of *Macbeth* or describing his impulse to add wood to the fire.

---

[48] *B.L.*, Vol. I, pp. 164–165.

VI. GENIUS

THE WIDESPREAD PRESENCE in Coleridge of the theory of organic unity is evidence of the emotional as well as the intellectual hold it had on him. Nowhere is there a clearer illustration of his application of this idea than in his discussions of genius. The definition given in *The Friend* is: "The first (genius) I use in the sense of most general acceptance, as the faculty which adds to the existing stock of power and knowledge by new views, new combinations; by discoveries not accidental but anticipated, or resulting from anticipation. In short, I define Genius, as originality in intellectual construction."[1] The man of genius, then, is he who is able to add to the stock of knowledge by originating new forms. In other words, he is the man who can take a single idea or appearance, that is, the core of any progressive growth, and follow it through its evolution of forming more and richer combinations until it comes to its predestined conclusion. The elements of originality and contribution to knowledge are intrinsic to this process. It is simply the way creation occurs. The element of the accidental cannot possibly enter. The potentiality of growth is within the units in its simplest state and the man who develops it not only shows what is really there but, in a sense, anticipates the logical end of the progression.

The definition is further explained in the *Anima Poetae*. Here the man of genius is one who, in placing things in a new light, unfolds them, so to speak, and shows the complexity and richness of relations and therefore of meaning that is in them. He takes objects which are familiar but nevertheless are seen by the common man only in an "unsorted" and "unpacked" condition, and not only reveals their structure, but to them adds light and relations. Compare the difference, says Coleridge, between a flower which everyone knows and the same flower painted by a man of genius.[2] There is a striking similarity between this passage and

---

[1] Edition of 1884, p. 384. See also Raysor, *op. cit.* Vol. I, p. 223.   [2] *A.P.*, p. 233.

the one from Bosanquet quoted above,[3] where in discussing form he writes, "When you push home your insight into the order and connection of parts, not leaving out the way in which this affects the parts themselves, then you find that the form becomes 'very material'; not merely outlines and shapes, but all the acts of gradations and variations and connections that make anything what it is—the life, soul, and movement of the object." By both men the stress is laid upon the insight into the structure of the thing. In Bosanquet the idea is grounded on a firmer philosophy, but as an instrument of criticism it is fundamentally the same as the theory held by Coleridge.

The relation to nature of the man of genius is discussed in "On Poesy and Art." The wisdom in nature is distinguished from the wisdom in man by the fact that in nature the plan and the execution, the thought and the product, are one, or are given at once; but man has freedom and choice. The thought and the product are not coinstantaneous. In man's mind are focused all the rays of intellect which are scattered throughout the images of nature. It is the work of the man of genius to place these images taken from nature, totalized and fitted to the limits of the human mind, in such a way that they reflect perfectly the structure of the inner spirit of nature; if this is done there will be a perfect union between the image and the idea for which it stands. As Coleridge says, the mystery of genius is "to make the external internal, the internal external, to make nature thought, and thought nature."[4] It is only when man by an act of genius is able to accomplish this that art has its best and, in the highest sense, most truthful expression.

In this combination of nature and thought, of the external with the internal, there is implicit the idea that man cannot merely copy nature; for if he did that he would produce a mask only, not a form breathing life. He must not copy; he must, rather, isolate himself from nature and out of his own mind "create forms according to the severe laws of the intellect."[5]

---

[3] See p. 40.   [4] *B.L.*, Vol. I, p. 258.   [5] *Ibid.*

If he is successful in creating these forms, he will then be "assimilated to nature" because the laws of the intellect are the same as the laws of nature and the creation of a form according to these laws will mean the creation of a form which is in nature. Only when the laws are evolved and he speaks the same language as nature may he approach her endless compositions of them.

There is, then, for each work of true genius an appropriate form.[6] Indeed, the form is the very soul of the work. "Appropriate" is a rather weak word because the work of genius cannot escape the form; it must be created according to the law. Here is Coleridge's answer to these critics who look upon Shakespeare as "a sort of African nature, fertile in beautiful monsters—as a wild heath where islands of fertility look greener from the surrounding waste."[7] The form of Shakespeare is the form of nature, and because his works have that form they are expressions of reality. The French dramatists such as Corneille and Racine, on the other hand, fail because the scheme they employ is mechanical. They do not look into nature and into their own minds to evolve the form; rather, they take a mechanical form and impress it as matrix upon the materials which come to their hands.

The close connection between Coleridge's theory of genius and his idea of organic unity must be apparent at once. Shakespeare was "a nature humanized, a genial understanding directing self-consciously a power and an implicit wisdom deeper even than our own consciousness."[8] "He worked in the spirit of nature, evolving the germ from within by the imaginative power according to an idea."[9] There is in Coleridge's expression of this theory a consistency of thought surprising in a man who is noted for his lack of it.

The theory of genius is further elaborated in the second chapter of the *Biographia,* in which Coleridge takes up the question of temperament. If a man is a genius, his ideas are vivid and he has an endless power of combining and modifying them. His

[6] Raysor, *op. cit.,* Vol. I, p. 223.   [8] *Ibid.,* p. 224.
[7] *Ibid.*   [9] *Works,* 1847 ed., Vol. XV, p. 43.

feelings and affections blend far more easily and intimately with these ideal creations than with the objects of sense; he is affected by thoughts rather than by things.

But there is a distinction which must be made between men of commanding and men of absolute genius. The men of absolute genius "rest content between thought and reality, as it were in an intermundium of which their own living spirit supplies the substance, and their imagination the ever varying form."[10] The man of genius discovers the structure of the world and so lives in a sphere which is different in kind from the sphere of ordinary men. The men of greatest genius appear to have been calm and tranquil in all that related to themselves. The man of commanding genius, on the other hand, is in a less happy state; the high calm is not for him. Such men "must impress their conceptions on the world without, in order to present them back to their own view with the satisfying degree of clearness, distinctness, and individuality." In tranquil times, such men are able to exhibit a perfect poem in a palace or a temple; but in times of tumult "they are destined . . . to destroy the wisdom of ages in order to substitute the fancies of a day."[11] These men are unreliable because, although they have at times the power of higher imagination, that power is sporadic and does not enable them to see consistently the essential form and order of the world. Beaumont and Fletcher might be called men of commanding genius, because they are able at times to present a perfect passage or scene; yet their works as a whole lack organic unity.

There is one further point to be made, a point which is in part a repetition of a comment on Shakespeare already discussed. It has to do with sensibility. A quick and deep sensibility "is not only a characteristic feature, but may be deemed a component part, of genius."[12] But this sensibility has nothing to do with the irritability attributed to great artists; for a man of absolute genius looks upon his personal affairs in exactly the same way that he looks upon things which are external to himself. His sensibility

---

[10] *B.L.*, Vol. I, p. 20.　　[11] *Ibid.*, p. 21.　　[12] *Ibid.*, p. 30.

is excited as quickly and as powerfully by the one as by the other. He "lives most in the ideal world, in which the present is still constituted by the future or the past; and because his feelings have been habitually associated with thoughts and images, to the number, clearness, and vivacity of which the sensation of self is always in an inverse proportion."[13] When a man lives on the plane of pure action, when his mind is constantly occupied in combining images in accordance with the structure of reality, the small everyday sensations of self lose their importance.

From the preceding pages it appears that Coleridge's theory of genius is not only wholly in accord with, but is an inseparable part of, his idea of organic unity. In short, the man of genius is he who is continuously able to bring to bear upon his material the power of higher imagination. Through his imagination he is able to discover the laws of nature and create works of art in accordance with those laws. In doing this he is not only revealing the essential order of the world, but is also adding new forms, new combinations of images to the stock of significant relations which the world of common experience possesses. The images which he uses in the creation of the forms are perfectly unified with the spirit they represent. As his genius is greater his small personal feelings of self are less; and as a result of his power of combining thoughts and images in accordance with the real order of the world he achieves a high calm.

---

[13] *B.L.*, Vol. I, p. 30.

VII. THEORY OF POETRY

O N VARIOUS OCCASIONS, both in the *Biographia* and in the
Lectures on Shakespeare, Coleridge gave definitions of
a poem. These definitions are in an almost word-for-word
agreement with one another and are all directly based on his
conception of organic unity. The first prerequisite of a poem is
that it have such unity. In the *Biographia* he writes: "A poem
is that species of composition, which is opposed to works of science, by proposing for its *immediate* object pleasure, not truth;
and from all other species (having this object in common with
it) it is discriminated by proposing to itself such delight from the
whole, as is compatible with a distinct gratification from each
component part."[1] Not only in this definition, but in each of the
others as well, poetry is opposed to science rather than to prose.
At bottom, the reason for this contrast lies in the criterion already
mentioned of judging any work by the end for which it was
intended.[2]

The end of poetry is pleasure; the end of science is truth; therefore these two, if not exact opposites, are at least distinctly different. Coleridge deliberately ignores prose because poetry and prose
are opposites only superficially as devices of expression, and because poetry as a way of apprehending experience may occur in
either prose or verse. When the distinction is grounded on the
way experience is apprehended, then the opposition between
poetry and science becomes the more truly descriptive one.

The organization of a poem is simply one expression of organic
unity. Each element is distinct in itself, and has some value even
when isolated; but the important factor is that each element must
bear its proper relation to the whole. The unity of a poem, for
example, may be spoiled by the very excellence of a figure of
speech which, standing out from its context, receives more attention than its relation to the whole poem warrants. Here again

---

[1] Vol. II, p. 10. See also Raysor, *op. cit.,* Vol. I, p. 164; Vol. II, pp. 67, 78, 98, 200.
[2] See above, p. 55.

is an example of practical criticism growing out of philosophical. The principle is peculiarly applicable to young poets who have the power at times of writing suddenly and in isolation a beautiful figure which juts out from the context of a poem. It is only natural that such a poet should look with skepticism upon a critical judgment which tells him to discard a figure because, so it seems, it is too good.

Considering the definition of a poem from a philosophical position, I wish to indicate a passage in Bosanquet which shows outstanding similarities. He writes: "A world or cosmos is a system of members, such that every member, being, ex hypothesi distinct, nevertheless contributes to the unity of the whole in virtue of the peculiarities which constitute its distinctness."[3] The similarity between this and Coleridge's definition of a poem is obvious. There is only one important difference. Bosanquet stresses the point that each member makes its contribution by virtue of the peculiarities which constitute its distinctness. Coleridge does not include this point explicitly in his definition, but it is everywhere implied in his discussions of poetry. It is the peculiar constitution of the elements which go to make up a poem: the meter, the emotion, the objects and incidents contemplated, and the relations between them which constitute its total nature. It is important to recognize that organic unity is not a form into which contents may be placed, but that it is a form, unique in value, which grows out of the nature and combination of its elements.

It is obvious that Coleridge's definition of a poem does not take meter into account. In his introduction to the definition in the *Biographia,* he correctly classifies meter as "superficial form."[4] But the problem cannot be dismissed so lightly. He brings up romances whose end is pleasure, and asks the question, "Would then the mere superaddition of meter, with or without rhyme, entitle these to the name of poems?" He continues: "The answer is, that nothing can permanently please which does not contain

---

[3] *Principle of Individuality and Value,* p. 37.   [4] *B.L.,* Vol. II, p. 9.

in itself the reason why it is so, and not otherwise. If meter be superadded all other parts must be made consonant with it."[5] The assumption here surely is that the subject must be apprehended in such a way as to make meter its natural form of expression. The same assumption, although possibly weaker, is in the corresponding passage in the *Lectures on Shakespeare*. Speaking of prose the end of which is pleasure, he writes, "Yet still neither we nor the writers call such work a poem, though no work could deserve that name which did not include all this, together with something else."[6] That "something else" of which he speaks is the power of poetry. In other words, that which really distinguishes a poem is a poetic way of apprehending life; meter is natural but not essential.

Having established the fact that meter is not essential, Coleridge makes an incomplete consideration of the position of meter. In the *Biographia* he writes, ". . . a poem of any length neither can be nor ought to be all poetry. Yet if an harmonious whole is to be produced, the remaining parts must be preserved *in keeping* with the poetry; and this can be no otherwise effected than by such a studied selection and artificial arrangement, as will partake of *one,* though not a peculiar property of poetry."[7] Although the word "meter" is not used in this passage, the phrase "studied selection and artificial arrangement" obviously can refer to nothing else. The conclusion, then, is that meter is one of the properties of poetry, but is not a necessary element. Although organic unity naturally inclines to metrical expression, it does not inevitably achieve it, except, perhaps, in its greatest possible force.

According to Coleridge's theory, a poem is the literary expression of that which is poetic. Any work of art, so far as it achieves the unity of which he is speaking, may be termed "poetry." Thus there may be poetry in a painting, a statue, or a musical composition. In fact, poetry and organic unity are in a sense synonymous. Passages in prose works not intended for pleasure may be

[5] *Ibid.*   [6] *Ibid.,* p. 11.   [7] *Ibid.*

poetic in the highest sense. Coleridge writes, "The writings of Plato and Bishop Taylor ... furnish undeniable proofs that poetry of the highest kind may exist without meter, and even without the contradistinguishing objects of a poem."[8] He wished a sure connection to be made between his definition of a poem and his theory of poetry and art in general. This is to be seen when he writes that "this most general and distinctive character of a poem originates in the poetic genius itself. ... it yet becomes a just ... definition of poetry in its highest and most peculiar sense, only so far as the distinction still results from the poetic genius, which sustains and modifies the emotions, thoughts, and vivid representations of the poem by the energy without effort of the poet's own mind."[9]

In the *Biographia,* Coleridge sees that "poetry" is a larger term than "poem" and so makes an attempt to describe its nature. However, he shifts his ground a trifle by asserting that the answer to "What is poetry?" is so nearly the same as the answer to "What is a poet?" that he will concern himself only with the latter question. The shift in ground is not important, for the discussion refers directly to the secondary imagination which is essential to his theory.

According to Coleridge, the poet is he who has secondary imagination and is enabled, by its power to bring "the whole soul of man into activity" and to "diffuse a tone and spirit of unity that blends, and (as it were) fuses each into each."[10] We notice that his language here is far from the artificiality of Schelling's progression of thesis, antithesis, and synthesis. Coleridge saw, rather, a growing blend and fusion of particulars in a work of art. He is using the older idiom again when he writes, "this power ... reveals itself in the balance or reconciliation of opposite or discordant qualities."[11] "Balance or reconciliation of opposites" is familiar language to a follower of Schelling or Fichte, but the word "discordant" brings a new note. If we admit a synthesis and new thesis from qualities which are merely discordant rather

---

[8] *B.L.*, Vol. II, p. 11.   [9] Raysor, *op. cit.*, Vol. I, p. 166.   [10] *B.L.*, Vol. II, p. 12.   [11] *Ibid.*

than opposite, the system of Schelling breaks down. That is not true, however, of Bosanquet, who stressed the growth of a central core which reached out and gathered in all relevant particulars whether they were opposite, similar, or discordant. It is only by the later philosophy that we can justify the series of particulars which Coleridge gives as being blended by the imaginative power. That series is as follows:

... of sameness with difference; of the general, with the concrete; the idea, with the image; the individual, with the representative; the sense of novelty and freshness, with old and familiar objects; a more than usual state of emotion, with more than usual order; judgment ever awake and steady self-possession, with enthusiasm and feeling profound or vehement; and while it blends and harmonizes the natural and the artificial, still subordinates art to nature; the manner to the matter; and our admiration of the poet to our sympathy with the poetry.[12]

When these things happen, Coleridge is saying, the result is poetry. Passages from Taylor or Plato evidence these things and so are poetry. Matthew Arnold felt rather than understood such an occurrence in his "touchstones." Coleridge does not enrich his series with illustrations, but merely concludes by saying that fancy is the drapery of poetic genius and imagination the soul. He means, I suppose, that drapery may be interesting, but is unimportant. Taken as a whole, his account of poetry is thoroughly in accord with his philosophical theory.

The centering of his mind upon an idealistic system of thought is illustrated by a characteristic aside in which he interprets Milton's phrase describing poetry as "simple, sensuous, and passionate." Milton tossed off his description as a mere subordinate clause, but Coleridge expands it for two pages. According to Coleridge, poetry is simple in that it presupposes a finished work, not an arduous process looking towards an end not yet arrived at; the reader moves smoothly through a poem. Also, simplicity precludes affectation and morbid peculiarity. Poetry is sensuous in that it has a framework of objectivity, a definiteness in articulation of imagery, and a modification of the images themselves. It

---

[12] *Ibid.*

is passionate in that neither thought nor imagery "shall be simply objective, but that the *passio vera* of humanity shall warm and animate both."[13] Coleridge's discussion of Milton's phrase is excellent as a general description of poetry. It is hardly possible, however, to allow him his assertion that Milton implied in the three words all that Coleridge had said in his discussion and definition of poetry. It is difficult to see how the idea of organic unity is implied in that phrase. What is very easy to see is the way in which Coleridge invested the words with the theory which was uppermost in his mind. The passage is of interest chiefly because it shows further evidence of a strong central thought running through his criticism.

The theory of poetry explained in the preceding pages was the result of a lifelong belief on the part of Coleridge that poetry had a logic of its own. He tells in the *Biographia* how at Christ's Hospital the Rev. Bowyer instilled this precept in him, adding that logic was "as severe as that of science and more difficult, because more subtle, more complex, and dependent on more and more fugitive causes."[14] As his experience with art and philosophy grew greater, he turned naturally to an idealistic system of thought, where he found what was to him the most satisfactory expression of that logic of poetry the existence of which he had, in his youth, apprehended, but the structure of which he had not understood. It was of the greatest importance to him that the philosophy of Kant was having its fullest effect, for there has rarely been a man whose natural abilities were so aptly constructed to take advantage of a new philosophy. Coleridge was thoroughly in accord with Fichte and Schelling, the romantic philosophers, in his desire for unity. That unity was all-embracing, and, so far as he was concerned, led directly to God. It is important to remember that the unity of a poem was essentially the same as the unity in nature and that the unity of anything in the universe was an expression of God; therefore a poem which achieved this organic unity was at the same time giving expression to truth.

---

[13] Raysor, *op. cit.*, Vol. I, p. 166.   [14] *B.L.*, Vol I, p. 4.

Nature, however, may not be used for a criterion of poetry any more than poetry may be used for a criterion of nature; each one is merely an expression of the total unity which constitutes the world. When Coleridge uses, or seems to use, nature as a criterion of poetry, he can only mean nature considered as the system of organic unity which he has described.

The theory of poetry which Coleridge held was greatly enriched by a series of critical dicta scattered throughout his works. These were not given as logical steps in the progression of a theory, and for that reason do not have an ordered development. They are all, however, definite expressions of the theory I have been speaking of.

The first of these dicta, which because of their haphazard order have been rather arbitrarily selected, is found in the *Biographia*. Coleridge writes, "Whatever lines can be translated into other words of the same language without diminution of their significance, either in sense or association, or in any worthy feeling, are so far vicious in their diction."[15] Here is a criterion which is at the same time a practical test for the most unphilosophical and a direct outgrowth of philosophical theory. The development of organic unity is fixed and unchangeable; the gathering of the materials which are unified is a process which is spontaneous, dynamic, and inevitable. The finished product is in no way open to substitution or change. If there should be change, that change would necessarily be a continuation of the process; it could never refer to what had already been accomplished. Applied to the greatest poetry, the principle is an aid in that it helps to define that greatness more clearly and at the same time more richly. Applied to poetry of undetermined merit, the principle is of value as a practical test. Coleridge writes that "it would be scarcely more difficult to push a stone out from the Pyramids with the bare hand, than to alter a word, or the position of a word, in Milton or Shakespeare (in their most important works at least) without making the author say something else, or something worse,

[15] *Ibid.*, p. 14.

then he does say."[16] When the form is once perfectly set, it is unchangeable. The rather absurd lengths to which an absolute
acceptance of this principle would carry the critic is an excellent
example of the dangers which beset any theory. The idea is both
sound and applicable to the material, but the dogmatic use of it is
likely to result in criticism of the museum variety.

The second of these dicta is found in the *Anima Poetae*. Coleridge writes, "The desire of carrying things to a greater height
of pleasure and admiration than, *omnibus-trutinatis,* they are
susceptible of, is one great cause of corruption of poetry."[17] Any
subject-matter has its appropriate expression. Any core or central
idea with which a work of art is begun has its proper development and conclusion. An attempt to give expression to more than
is intrinsic in any subject will not only result in dissatisfaction
with the manner of expression, but will also take away from what
value the subject originally had. The words formerly applied to
such an attempt are "bombast" on the one hand and "sentimentality" on the other, although sentimentality is all-inclusive if
it is taken to mean any emotion which is greater than is justified
by the situation from which it arises. Coleridge continues by
thinking of Catullus and wondering if it is *possible* for Ovid or
Tibullus to express the same ideas as those of Catullus but in a
different meter. The answer is, obviously, No. Whenever it has
been tried, the result has been to substitute manner for matter,
changing the idea itself. The same fault is charged to Pope, particularly in "the cold blooded use, for artifice or connection, of
language justifiable only by enthusiasm and passion."[18] Such a
use is a corruption in that either it arouses emotions or associations which are incongruous with the context, or else it is flat and
colorless according to the context and is robbed of the meaning
which is rightfully inherent in it.[19]

The third of these dicta was repeated in various forms many

[16] B.L., Vol. I, p. 15.   [17] A.P., p. 165.   [18] Ibid., p. 166.
[19] This dictum was a favorite with ancient critics and rhetoricians, notably Longinus.
The agreements of different critics with varying backgrounds are more significant than
their disagreements.

times by Coleridge. It amounts, in short, to the principle that criticism should be positive rather than negative; that it should apply itself chiefly to the beauties and excellences of a work rather than to the defects. In the *Anima Poetae* we find this principle in its most extreme form: "Never to lose an opportunity of reasoning against the ... principle of judging a work by its defects, not by its beauties. Every work must have the former—we know it a priori—but every work has not the latter, and he therefore, who discovers them tells you something that you could not with certainty, or even with probability, have anticipated."[20] The positive element in this passage is reinforced by another remark in the same book: "Men's intellectual errors consist chiefly in denying. What they affirm with feeling is for the most part, right."[21] Idealistic thought is markedly positive rather than negative. It is an affirmation of the nature and structure of the world. So it is entirely logical that the critic who uses the principles of that thought should, after largely identifying value with the presence of those principles, spend his effort in a search for the idealistic structure in the work which he is criticizing. Although the display of beauties may in one sense be the most valuable function which the critic can perform, it can hardly be taken as a complete statement of the aim of criticism. Coleridge realized the one-sidedness of such an aim and modified his point of view in the *Biographia.* There he lays the greatest stress upon discovering what is really characteristic of an author. He was particularly irritated by the habit of contemporary reviewers of deciding on the merit of a work by accidental failures or faulty passages. You might as well, he writes, quote as a fair specimen of Milton's sonnets, "A book was writ of late called Tetrachordon."[22] If you must choose defects to write of, choose those which are characteristic because they will lead to characteristic beauties. In general, he placed the emphasis upon the beauties of a work and upon the defects which were closely bound up with those beauties. Irrelevant defects were merely irrelevant and therefore not worth writ-

---

[20] *A.P.*, p. 30.   [21] *Ibid.*, p. 147.   [22] *B.L.*, Vol. I, p. 44.

ing about. He himself followed this dictum in his analysis of Wordsworth when he apologized for speaking of the defects first, saying that he had already expressed himself on the subject of Wordsworth's poetry with such fullness as to preclude ill effects which might otherwise arise from such an arraignment.[23] In the analysis itself it is the characteristic excellences which are emphasized; the defects are shown to be minor and comparatively unimportant.

The fourth of these dicta is not so explicitly worked out as those which I have already discussed, but is perhaps more interesting so far as it relates to later developments in idealism. To use Bosanquet's phrase, this dictum may be stated as the distinction between easy and difficult beauty. In the *Anima Poetae,* Coleridge writes: "The elder languages were fitter for poetry because they expressed only prominent ideas with clearness, the others but darkly.... Poetry gives most pleasure when only generally and not perfectly understood."[24] In other words, the great poetry of the ancients had a strong central core which it was easy to follow, but elaborating and enriching this core were many less important ideas difficult to grasp. The greatness of that poetry depended to some degree upon the reaching out of the reader's mind into a continually better understanding of the totality of the ideas, and the relationships which existed between them. Ease of comprehension and immediacy of response are never to be taken as criteria of greatness in poetry. Mere excitement without what Coleridge calls reaction is not only valueless, but actually harmful; for "Poetry which excites us to artificial feelings makes us callous to real ones."[25] Coleridge expressed the same idea in a slightly different form in another passage in the *Biographia* when he wrote, "Quaere, whether or no too great definiteness of terms in any language may not consume too much of the vital and idea-creating force in distinct, clear, full-made images and so prevent originality."[26] Great precision of language will inevitably restrict the dynamic force of images and will thus tend

---

[23] *B.L.,* Vol. II, p. 97.   [24] *A.P.,* p. 5.   [25] *Ibid.*   [26] *Ibid.,* p. 19.

to make poorer the possibilities of extension which are in them. Coleridge might have gone on to show that it is exactly the opposite with science, where precision is the highest aim and the meaning of the words should be static, not dynamic.

The passages quoted above support the critical aphorism which Coleridge gives in the *Biographia:* "Not the poem which we have read, but that to which we return, with the greatest pleasure, possesses the genuine power, and claims the name of essential poetry."[27] The poem which does not grow in power and beauty for us with each reading is by this test condemned as easy, and superficial in significance.

The distinction between easy and difficult beauty involved here was made far more explicitly by Bosanquet in his *Three Lectures on Aesthetic.* With neither Coleridge nor Bosanquet is easy beauty unaesthetic; it is merely on a lower level. It is the kind which is pleasant to nearly everyone. Examples Bosanquet gives are a simple tune, a rose, or a youthful face. Difficult beauty is so named because of the difficulty of apprehending it. Characteristics of this kind of beauty given by Bosanquet are intricacy, tension, and width.[28] I shall use an example of intricacy. A musically uneducated person listening to a great symphony will at the first hearing be unable to grasp it as a work of art. There are parts of it, however, which he will be able to grasp: the sensuous beauty of the instruments; the simple statement of the melody. These parts represent easy beauty. But if he hears it often enough he will gradually come to an understanding of the intricate whole; the way the theme is modified, broken up, restated, and played by different instruments; the relation of the various movements, with their peculiar tempos, to one another; the use and relation of the characteristic timbres of the different instruments; the possibilities of different interpretations of the score, and, more specifically, the interpretation which the present conductor is giving it. In understanding these things which were formerly unknown to him, he will be coming into contact with difficult beauty. At his

---

[27] Vol. I, p. 14.   [28] *Three Lectures,* p. 97.

first hearing of the symphony he may be rather bored; at best it will seem a little confused and disordered even though the emotional impact is great. But at his most mature hearing he will enjoy not only the easy beauty which he first enjoyed, but also all the extensive materials and relationships which go to make up its total organization. In this development of appreciation, the auditor is himself going through the process of organic unity, from the simple appearances with which his knowledge began to the extended but closely knit relationships with which it was completed. The passages I have quoted from Coleridge give evidence that he saw the application of this principle to poetry without being able to express it completely.

The fifth of these critical dicta is concerned with poetic diction. Coleridge discussed this subject at greater length than the others I have been speaking of, centering his remarks in Chapters XVII, XVIII, and XIX of the *Biographia*. His aim there was double-edged: first to refute Wordsworth's theory, and then to set up his own. The discussion originates, therefore, in an examination of Wordsworth's preface. It will be remembered that in general Wordsworth's contentions were that the proper diction for poetry was the language taken from the mouths of men in real life, in a state of excitement, and that this language was found best exemplified in low and rustic life. Diction so chosen, however, was subject to purification. The answer Coleridge gives to this is thoroughly characteristic of his philosophy. It is as follows: The language of a rustic "will not differ from the language of any other man of common-sense, however learned or refined he may be except as far as the notions, which the rustic has to convey are fewer and more indiscriminate."[29] That difference, however, is of the highest importance and contains the grounds on which Wordsworth's theory is refuted. For the rustic "aims almost solely to convey insulated facts, either those of his scanty experience or his traditional belief." The educated man, on the contrary, is interested chiefly in discovering connections or relations of things

---

[29] *B.L.*, Vol. II, p. 39.

"from which some more or less general law is deducible."[30] Facts are valuable only so far as they lead to the discovery of law which is the true being of things. The opposition of fact to relation which leads to the discovery of law is wholly in accord with idealism in its most modern development. Taken alone, facts are static, isolated, lacking in significance. It is only when the imagination, working upon them, discovers their organic relationship that there can be any form or meaning. Value can be attributed to facts only when they are part of a structure—in short, the structure of organic unity. The best part of human language, therefore, "is derived from reflection on the acts of the mind itself. It is formed by a voluntary appropriation of fixed symbols to internal acts, to processes and results of imagination."[31] The mind of the rustic has little or no training in the expression of relations. There is "disjunction and separation in the component parts of that, whatever it be, which they wish to communicate."[32] They are denied that grasp of the connections of things leading into an organized whole which becomes a spontaneous process in the mind of an educated man. In short, their lack of experience denies them the apprehension of organic unity. This was concretely expressed by Coleridge in a passage very similar to one by Walter Pater which appears in his essay on style. Coleridge says: "There is a want [in the rustics] of that prospectiveness of mind, that surview, which enables a man to foresee the whole of what he is to convey, appertaining to any one point; and by this means so to subordinate and arrange the different parts according to their relative importance, as to convey it at once, and as an organized whole."[33]

It is clear that the unity Coleridge attributed to the educated man is merely one aspect of organic unity. The question of whether or not the interest in relations leads to truth is here irrelevant; it is sufficient that such an interest exists, for it is the only road to truth. The consistency Coleridge showed in making this distinction between the educated and the uneducated man is strength-

---

[30] *Ibid.*   [31] *Ibid.*, pp. 39–40.   [32] *Ibid.*, p. 44.   [33] *Ibid.*

ened by a passage from *The Friend*: "It is the unpremeditated and evidently habitual arrangement of his words, grounded on the habit of foreseeing in each integral part, or (more plainly) in every sentence, the whole that he then intends to communicate. However irregular and desultory his talk, there is method in the fragments."[34] It is to be observed that Coleridge here considers method as so thoroughly impregnating a mind that structure is noticeable even in short remarks.

The passage last quoted leads him to a further explanation of unity which holds good for modern idealists. His point is that the process is one which has no relation to time. Unity does not mean mere regularity, of which a clock is capable. The man of methodical industry "realizes (time's) ideal divisions and gives a character and individuality to its moments. . . . He takes up (time) into his own permanence and communicates to it the imperishableness of a spiritual nature. . . . It is less truly affirmed that he lives in time, than that time lives in him."[35] Time can lend no justifiable order to events, cannot contain unity in its mere sequence. It is nothing but the abstract framework in which events happen. It may, however, be regarded as one of the materials of art, and in spite of its essential transitory nature be so organized as to gain permanence and significance.

In his discussion of Wordsworth's theory, Coleridge has been, one might say, fair rather to his own philosophy than to Wordsworth. The distinction between fact and relation with the value given to relation played no part at all in Wordsworth's preface, and indeed could hardly have been understood in its philosophical implications by that poet. Coleridge's method of argument shifted the grounds to a field in which Wordsworth was not prepared to answer. Victory was here so certain for Coleridge that it was not worth while to continue the dispute. On one side there was the man of common sense, Wordsworth, expounding a view which in its general effect upon English poetry was of great value; on the other side, the philosopher, who saw the unsoundness of

---

[34] P. 409.   [35] *Ibid.*

the view, denied it any validity, gave his reasons, and then developed his answer according to a philosophy in such a way that the reply went far beyond the original objective. Once Coleridge had reduced Wordsworth's theory to a reliance upon isolated facts, he was able to reconstruct it along the lines of dynamic progression, which means, of course, organic unity.

The second point in Wordsworth's preface to which Coleridge objected was the assertion, "There neither is, nor can be, any essential difference between the language of prose and that of metrical composition."[36] So far as words alone are concerned, Coleridge emphatically believed that there was no difference between prose and metrical poetry. "Produce me one word," he writes, "out of Klopstock, . . . Schiller, Goethe, etc., which I will not find as frequently used in the most energetic prose writers."[37] That there have been words exclusively used in poetry is the result either of a situation in which there were a few literary men in a large society, as in Italy from Dante to Metastasio,[38] or one in which men have foolishly and artificially copied inappropriate words, as when the Venetians imitated the Tuscanisms of Dante. It is this artificial copying of words which causes the growth of what Coleridge calls "a garden of language" where "all the showy and all the odorous words and clusters of words are brought together, and to be plucked by mere mechanic and passive memory."[39] The fact that there was no distinction between words used in poetry or prose was implicit in Coleridge's exposition of the difference between the language of the rustic and of the educated man.

If, however, we consider the difference between poetry and prose so far as style is concerned, the question becomes, Are there modes of expression which are proper in prose but which would be disproportionate in poetry, and vice versa?[40] The affirmative answer which Coleridge gives here is concerned with the nature of meter. According to his analysis, meter originated from the natural and spontaneous effort of the mind to control passion.

[36] *B.L.*, Vol. II, p. 45.   [37] *A.P.*, p. 229.   [38] *Ibid.*   [39] *Ibid.*
[40] The following discussion is based on *B.L.*, Vol. II, pp. 49–50.

This control developed into meter through a conscious act of the will which endeavored to restrict and give form to the passion for the purpose of pleasure. Implicit in this is the idealistic notion that pleasure comes from the organization of passion into form, rather than from the passion per se. When meter is successfully used, these two elements, passion and will, must be synthesized or fused into a whole. This fusion can be manifested only "in a frequency of forms and figures of speech (originally the offspring of passion but now the adopted children of power) greater than would be desired or endured, where the emotion is not voluntarily encouraged and kept up for the sake of that pleasure which such emotion, so tempered and mastered by the will, is found capable of communicating."[41] A figure is the child of power because it is in figures that the poet demonstrates his ability in minutiae to see and express the relations inherent in his material by reason of his imaginative power. The difference between metrical poetry and prose, so far as the origin of meter is affected, lies in a more continuous statement of passion and a greater profusion of figures in the former.

In this analysis Coleridge has resorted almost entirely to the Schelling system of reconciliation of antitheses. Passion and will are to be taken as opposites whose synthesis lies in the expression of a poem. Correctly interpreted, this does not mean that meter gives form to passion, but that both passion and meter grow into a form which is interpenetrated by each. The analysis, however, takes into account only two of the larger elements which go into the makeup of a total poem, and it is by no means certain that these two elements which are fused are exact opposites. It is not inconceivable that meter is an expression of passion per se. What is absolutely necessary is that there be a perfect fusion of the two elements, whatever the degree of their differences may be.

Meter, in its effects, contributes to the growing totality of a poem by stimulating both feelings and attention through the continual excitement of surprise and the arousing and gratifying

41 *B.L.*, Vol. II, p. 49.

of curiosity. Although the effect of these things may be too small to bring them to distinct consciousness, their aggregate is nevertheless powerful. Coleridge compares them to "wine during an animated conversation."[42] Here again is the principle of organic growth; at any given point the effect will include all that has gone before, and when the poem is finished its unity will consist in the perfect blending and fusion of all the elements which have gone into its being—not only the meter considered as will, and the contents as passion, but all the varying incidents, figures, degrees of passion, and variations of meter, besides.

Considered in its barest essentials, meter is simply a stimulant of the attention. The argument discussed in the preceding paragraph is a fair account of the effects of meter, but is hardly a criterion for distinguishing poetry from prose. Coleridge must have realized this, for he says that the answer to the question "Why is the attention to be thus stimulated?" can only be "I write in meter, because I am about to use a language different from that of prose."[43] The mere statement of such an answer is stronger, philosophically, than it seems to be. He is harking back, here, to his original distinction between poetry and science as pleasure and truth. For the idealist, the fundamental difference between these two is that they have different cores. The explanation of that difference is to be found in Coleridge's accounts of poetry considered as a whole.

The relation between meter and poetry is rendered more clear when Coleridge writes that meter is "the proper form of poetry, and poetry [is] imperfect and defective without meter."[44] I do not take this to be a denial of the poetry which he asserted was in Plato and Jeremy Taylor; rather, I take him to mean that a *poem,* as merely *one* of the many forms poetry may assume, has its proper and appropriate expression in meter. The reason a poem is called defective without meter is that a poem presupposes a continuous state of excitement, and that the characteristic expression of such a state is metrical. This argument, however, must

---

[42] *Ibid.,* p. 51.   [43] *Ibid.,* p. 53.   [44] *Ibid.,* p. 55.

look for its support to his theory of the origin of meter; for that supplies the only answer to the question, "Why is meter characteristic of poetry?"

Coleridge concludes his arguments for the difference between the language of poetry and the language of prose with a passage which is strikingly similar to his definition of a poem: "I adduce the high spiritual instinct of the human being impelling us to seek unity by harmonious adjustment, and thus establishing the principle that all the parts of an organized whole must be assimilated to the more important and essential parts."[45] In other words, poetry is different from prose because the organization is different. That organization finds its proper, but not its necessary, expression in meter. Coleridge's arguments would be clearer if he were more definite about the meaning of "prose." Although he never makes the point explicitly, there can be little doubt that he identifies prose with science, that is, science regarded as an organization different in kind from poetry.

In the argument about meter and the language of poetry as a whole, as in the argument about the rustic and the educated man, Coleridge is being fairer to his philosophy than to Wordsworth. Wordsworth was not arguing against meter, and never wrote an unmetrical composition which he would call a poem. He was arguing, rather, against a stilted, outworn, and artificial diction in poetry. The looseness of his statement, combined with his unphilosophical approach, made him an easy victim for Coleridge.

The ultimate reliance of Coleridge upon his philosophy is nowhere more clearly brought out than in his remark that these arguments (the ones mentioned above) might "be strengthened by the reflection, that the composition of a poem is among the imitative arts; and that imitation, as opposed to copying, consists either in the interfusion of the same throughout the radically different, or of the different throughout a base radically the same."[46] That is, imitation correctly interpreted is simply the process of organic unity. Coleridge's statement of the principle as "the in-

[45] *B.L.*, Vol. II, p. 56.   [46] *Ibid.*

terfusion of the same throughout the radically different" is directly paralleled by Bosanquet, who says of unity, "The ultimate principle, we may say, is sameness in the other; generality is sameness in spite of the other; universality is sameness by means of the other."[47] Any core or identity in its growth tends to include more relevant appearances and thus achieves sameness or identity in appearances which were formerly different. Bosanquet writes, "It [the test of the universal] is the degree in which a systematic identity subordinates diversity to itself, or more truly, reveals itself as the spirit of communion and totality, within which identity and difference are distinguishable but inseparable points of view."[48] This is simply a statement of organic unity in terms emphasizing identity.

It must be understood that in his arguments about the difference between the diction of prose and the diction of poetry Coleridge is taking the highest view of poetry. He is speaking of great poets and of the greatest things of which poetry is capable. He himself recognized, however, that there was poetry in existence, different and lesser in kind than the greatest, which still had distinct value. He commends Garve for best characterizing this poetry as "verses in which everything was expressed just as one would wish to talk, and yet all dignified, attractive and interesting; and all at the same time perfectly correct as to the measure of the syllables and the rhyme."[49] "These verses," Coleridge continues, "are specimens of that style which, as the neutral ground of prose and verse, is common to both."[50] Daniel, Spenser, Chaucer, and Herbert afford many examples of this style. Valuable as it may be, it is at best a "milder muse" and is the result of observation and good taste rather than imagination. In short, its only defect is that it lacks the greatest value that verse can have: a poetic apprehension of reality.

The sixth of these critical dicta consists of the group of specific symptoms of poetic power discussed by Coleridge in Chapter XV of the *Biographia.* There as before we shall see that the materials

---

[47] *Individuality and Value*, p. 29.   [48] *Ibid.*, p. 40.   [49] *B.L.*, Vol. II, p. 70.   [50] *Ibid.*

of practical criticism grow directly out of his philosophical theory. He chooses Shakespeare's *Venus and Adonis* as a work appropriate for analysis for the reason that it was an early production of a great poet. The most obvious excellence of that poem is its versification, which shows sweetness, is perfectly adapted to the subject, and is varied without being disproportionate. "The sense of musical delight," Coleridge continues, "with the power of producing it is a gift of the imagination."[51] It may be cultivated, but never can be learned. The imagination is called into play here because it is through that faculty that a great poet is able to give passion a form distinctively musical, that is, melodic, harmonic, as well as metrical. The seemingly obvious fact that musical delight is one of the essential elements in that fusion of experience called poetry has been too often overlooked. Coleridge here as frequently elsewhere demands a richer attentiveness to the factors involved.

The second symptom of poetic power is a "choice of subjects very remote from the private interests and circumstances of the writer himself."[52] The argument for this has already been given in substance.[53] The writer who uses his personal sensations and experiences as material and merely expresses the things through which he has lived is narrowly limited because his individuality is an effect and not a power. The imaginative power which enables a man to reproduce the universal in a work of art works upon all appearances as substances capable of endless modification; of all these appearances his own personality is but one particular. It is for this reason that in *Venus and Adonis* we seem to feel that a "superior spirit more intuitive, more intimately conscious, even than the characters themselves, not only of every outward look and act, but of the flux and reflux of the mind in all its subtlest thoughts and feelings,"[54] is placing the whole before our view. The author himself is not participating in the passions; he is the mere agent in which the creative process takes place spontaneously.

[51] *B.L.,* Vol. II, p. 14.   [52] *Ibid.*   [53] See above, p. 46.   [54] *B.L.,* Vol. II, p. 14.

According to Coleridge, the subject-matter of *Venus and Adonis* is morally dangerous, but the process of Shakespeare's creation rendered it harmless. This is an interesting example of the working of organic unity. The animal impulse is central to the poem and must have an important place in it. Ariosto and Wieland both saw the poem as expressing that impulse chiefly, and organized their material in such a way as to make it predominant. With Shakespeare, however, the meanness of the animal impulse is destroyed through the extensive relationships into which the poem grows; the dress, the scenery, the reflections originated by the incidents—all these force the reader into an activity which prevents him from sinking into the low and easily sensual. For the idealist, great art, let its subject-matter be what it may, cannot be immoral.

The third symptom of power is in the quality of the images which a poet creates. It is possible for a poet to make an image through mere copying from nature, book, or travel; indeed, images are most frequently of this sort. These, however, do not contain the essence of poetry. Coleridge writes, "They [images] become proofs of original genius only as far as they are modified by a predominant passion; or by associated thoughts or images awakened by that passion; or when they have the effect of reducing multitude to unity, or succession to an instant; or lastly, when a human and intellectual life is transferred to them from the poet's own spirit."[55] This series of tests represents different ways of applying the criterion of organic unity to a figure. The first two items refer specifically to the central idea of the poem. In order to be valuable, the image must be a modification and extension of that idea. "Multitude to unity, or succession to an instant" refers to the form-giving power of images. An image is in itself an apprehension of the relevance between things apparently different; and in bringing elements together and thus extending the totality of the poem the image creates the form. By the transference of a human and intellectual life from the

[55] *Ibid.*, p. 16.

poet's own spirit, Coleridge means that the poet has seen in nature
the working of that dynamic progression in which he himself
participates—in short, a spirit which for Coleridge was an emanation from God.

As an example of an image which "bursts upon us at once in
full life and power" he quotes the first two lines of the Shakespearean sonnet:

> Full many a glorious morning I have seen
> *Flatter* the mountain tops with sovereign eye.[56]

He does not comment, but I suppose that he saw expressed in
those lines the union of sunlight and mountain top made more
striking by the word "flatter," which, in blending the two, seems
to interfuse power and beauty into each. There is a suggestion
of grandeur in the early sun on the mountains, and a note of
mystery and power in the "sovereign eye" which moves and
causes these things to be. All are brought together, creating a
whole.

Again, as an image which reduces succession to an instant, he
quotes the lines from *Venus and Adonis:*

> With this, he breaketh from the sweet embrace
> Of those fair arms, which bound him to her breast,
> And homeward through the dark laund runs apace;—
> *Look! how a bright star shooteth from the sky,*
> So glides he in the night from Venus' eye.[57]

The succession of events, the breaking away by Adonis and the
running through the "dark laund" which gives the reader a
sense of the passage of time, is caught in an instant by the figure
of the bright star.

The fourth symptom of power is closely linked with the third;
it consists in depth and energy of thought.[58] Depth and energy
should be continuous; a single image may display these qualities,
but if it stands as an isolated peak the power which is promised
is only that of "transitory flashes." In this criterion we have one

---

[56] *B.L.*, Vol. II, p. 17.   [57] *Ibid.*, p. 18.   [58] *Ibid.*, p. 19.

of the leading ideas of Coleridge's thought: that poetry and philosophy go hand in hand. "No man was ever yet a great poet, without being at the same time a profound philosopher. For poetry is the blossom and the fragrance of all human knowledge, human thoughts, human passions, emotions, language."[59] It is entirely logical that Coleridge should say this, for, according to his theory, poetry and philosophy are simply different ways of apprehending truth. The process of unity which Shakespeare exhibited in *Lear* is the poetic and dramatic presentation of the same thing which a true philosopher expresses intellectually. There is only one truth, but there are many ways of reaching it.

In general we are justified in saying that Coleridge's account of poetry is thoroughly idealistic in nature and is to be understood only with reference to his philosophy. If we fail to take into account the metaphysical background, we are left with only isolated dicta, brilliant and revealing in themselves, perhaps, but still isolated. His first analysis of poetry, opposing poetry to science, is correct in the view of later idealists, although his use of the word "truth" was a little unfortunate in that the truly poetic must necessarily reveal truth. For the later idealist, the field of poetry is the field of art in general, whatever its mode of expression may be. Science is categorially different, since it works upon words taken conceptually rather than emotionally. In this latter distinction as well as in describing a poet and the nature of poetry, and in defining a poem, Coleridge was entirely consistent. His discussions of meter at times seem confused, but taken as a whole they are correct. There was no place in his philosophy for meter as a differentia of poetry, and he avoids using it as such.

[59] *Ibid.*

VIII. DRAMATIC CRITICISM

THE COLLECTED critical writings of Coleridge present to the ordinary reader a maze of repetition, digression, even occasional incoherency, in which are embedded thoughts the creative brilliance of which is a sufficient compensation for the arduous task of discovery. Until recently, the apparent formlessness of the material was aggravated by the lack of a thoroughly satisfactory edition of the highly important Shakespearean criticism. That problem, however, was solved by Professor T. M. Raysor, whose recent editing of all the material pertaining to Shakespeare is immensely superior in its accurate scholarship to any of the earlier collections. But in spite of the fullness and clarity with which the work is presented, the ideas themselves remain obscure and diverse unless they are understood as emanating from a single point of view, in short, from Coleridge's conception of organic unity. That is the only form we can expect from Coleridge. I have already indicated the growth and expression of the conception, and I will endeavor in the following pages to demonstrate his use of it in the criticism of specific works.

According to Coleridge, "Hamlet was the play, or rather Hamlet himself was the character in the intuition and exposition of which I first made my turn for philosophical criticism."[1] Therefore it is to *Hamlet* that we should look for evidences of his theory. If Coleridge looked upon *Hamlet* as an embodiment of the principle of organic unity, we must first discover what is the core of the growth which is to go through the process of expansion. In the largest sense, the core will consist of all the characters and circumstances with which the play begins. But more specifically the center of that core lies in a particular maladjustment in the character of Hamlet. According to Coleridge, there should be a balance "between our attention to outward objects and our meditation on inward thoughts." He continues: "In Hamlet this bal-

---

[1] Raysor, *op. cit.*, Vol. I, p. 18.

ance does not exist—his thoughts, images, and fancy [being] far more vivid than his perceptions, and his very perceptions instantly passing through the medium of his contemplations, and acquiring as they pass a form and color not naturally their own. Hence great, enormous, intellectual activity, and a consequent proportionate aversion to real action, with all its symptoms and accompanying qualities."[2] The statement is a conclusion; but it is also—and this is more important—a starting point. It may be considered as a hypothetical analysis of the play, the proof of which will lie in the ultimate extent of its relevance. Having determined the core, Coleridge had before him the task of demonstrating the working out of that core into the totality which is the play, *Hamlet*. It is in this work that his psychological insight combined with his emotional understanding of literature is of the greatest value to him, being made, as it is, the instrument of a philosophical theory.

The process of exhibiting the play in relation to its particular core is skillfully carried out so far as it shows the consistency with which Hamlet is unable to act in spite of his natural energy and the pressing need which is making demands upon it. Coleridge comments upon the judgment shown by Shakespeare in making the ghost real instead of a hallucination, and thus adding to the pressure on Hamlet by strengthening his motive.[3] He stresses the strong sense of duty which also adds to the conflict.[4] He enlarges his criticism by disagreeing with Dr. Johnson in two particulars: first, about the interpretation of the scene where Hamlet enters the church and finds his uncle praying; and second, on the subject of the voyage to England.[5] On both of these occasions the character is explained on the basis of an excess of thought with a consequent aversion to action. The consistency of the character is maintained in the tragic conclusion which is the result of chance.

There is only one objection to be made to this criticism, and that is, not that the method is poor, but that Coleridge failed to

---

[2] *Ibid.*, p. 37. The brackets are Raysor's.   [4] *Ibid.*, pp. 193–194.
[3] *Ibid.*, p. 193.   [5] *Ibid.*, pp. 196–197.

take full advantage of his method. It is rather surprising that he did not elaborate more fully what would be, to an idealist, the outstanding merit of the play: the way in which all the elements of the drama, the characters and their actions, center around and are the result of the core which is Hamlet, thus adding (in the idealistic sense) to the *individuality* of the protagonist and welding originally diverse elements into an organic whole.

As a contrast to the essential slowness of movement in *Hamlet,* a slowness springing from the nature of Hamlet's mind and the way in which it relates the action to itself, Coleridge cites *Macbeth.* In the latter play, "the invocation is made at once to the imagination and the emotions connected therewith."[6] "The Weird Sisters [set] the keynote of the character of the whole play."[7] Their mysterious evil power lay in tempting those who had already been tempters of themselves. Without them, Macbeth would have had a moral weakness, but the necessity of the tragic evolution would have been lacking. The original situation, or set of appearances from which the tragedy started, consisted in the influence of the Weird Sisters over the susceptible nature of Macbeth. Coleridge writes, ". . . if he yielded to the temptation and thus forfeited his free-agency, then the link of *cause* and *effect more physico* would commence."[8]

Given this core, or central point, Coleridge develops it consistently through textual comments. He contrasts Banquo's innocent curiosity about the Sisters with Macbeth's preoccupation and interest in order to demonstrate that the guilt is in its germ anterior to the supposed cause and immediate temptation. He shows that Macbeth's attitude toward Duncan contains nothing but the "commonplaces of loyalty"[9] in which he hides himself in the air. He explains the character who is "powerful in all things, but has strength in none."[10] Throughout the play, he interprets Macbeth as mistranslating "the recoilings and ominous whispers of conscience into prudential and selfish reasonings, and after the deed,

6 Raysor, *op. cit.,* Vol. I, p. 67.   8 *Ibid.*   10 *Ibid.,* p. 71.
7 *Ibid.,* p. 68. The brackets are Raysor's.   9 *Ibid.,* p. 70.

the terrors of remorse [are mistranslated] into fear from external dangers."[11]

In a fragment, Coleridge applies his theory of the imagination to Macbeth. Macbeth has hope, "which is the master element of a commanding genius, an active and combining intellect, and imagination of just that degree of vividness which disquiets and impels the soul to try to realize its images." That particular degree of genius Coleridge has already described in the *Biographia,* where he wrote that such men "must impress their preconceptions on the world without, in order to present them back to their own view with the satisfying degree of clearness, distinctness, and individuality."[12] Such a man is Macbeth. If his imaginative power had been greater, the images would have become a satisfying world of themselves, and we would have had a poet or original philosopher. But hope fully gratified turns to fear when the elementary basis of the passion still continues.

This latter criticism of Macbeth is apart from his comments on the play as a whole. When we take into consideration his complete criticism of the play, the most striking feature is his emphasis upon the hypothetical analysis and his careful demonstration of it in the earlier acts. He seems to imply that once the nature and course of growth is explained, an understanding of the complete development will follow naturally.

In his criticism of *Lear,* Coleridge uses one of his most characteristic principles, namely, that in the serious dramas of Shakespeare the interest and situations are never derived from a gross improbability. *Lear* is only a seeming and not a real exception to this. Coleridge writes, "Let the first scene of *Lear* have been lost, and let it be only understood that a fond father had been duped by hypocritical professions of love and duty on the part of two daughters to disinherit a third, previously, and deservedly, more dear to him, and all the rest of the tragedy would retain its interest undiminished and be perfectly intelligible."[13] In other

[11] *Ibid.,* p. 80. The brackets are Raysor's.
[12] Vol. I, p. 20.   [13] Raysor, *op. cit.,* Vol. I, p. 59.

words, the accidental is nowhere the basis of the passions, as it almost always is with Beaumont and Fletcher, whose plays are "founded on some out-of-the-way accident or exception to the general experience of mankind."[14] It is because of his apprehension of the pattern in nature that Shakespeare avoids artificiality and, in spite of the apparent improbability in the story of *Lear,* achieves organic unity. Coleridge supports his contentions about the "accidental" nature of the division of the kingdom by showing in the opening lines of the play that "the trial is but a trick; and that the grossness of the old king's rage is in part the natural result of a silly trick suddenly and most unexpectedly baffled and disappointed."[15]

Coleridge's account of the character of Lear is an interesting example of the application of his theory. Lear is taken as representing, centrally, old age, which is in itself a character.[16] The natural imperfections are increased by the lifelong habit of being promptly obeyed. Given this as the basis, Lear is distinguished by the relations of others to him. Thus we see the idealistic process of a character receiving individuality through his growing relations to others which, in adding to him, become a part of him. Coleridge saw in the growth of this character that Lear "is the open and ample play-room of Nature's passions."[17] We see in his first speeches the one general sentiment of ingratitude. Around this feeling the character of Lear is developed, in the first stages under pressure from the outward object because his mind is not yet sufficiently familiarized with the anguish for the imagination to work upon it.[18]

It is in accordance with the idea of organic growth that the Fool is brought into the play in such a way as to show his relation to the central core. Coleridge writes, "He is *prepared* for—brought into living connection with the pathos of the play, with the sufferings." This is achieved in the line,

Since my young lady's [going into France, sir, the fool hath much pined away.] (Act I, sc. 4.)[19]

---

[14] Raysor, Vol. I, p. 59.   [15] *Ibid.,* p. 55.   [16] *Ibid.,* p. 62.   [17] *Ibid.*   [18] *Ibid.,* p. 63.   [19] *Ibid.*

Again, in this play Coleridge follows his usual method of giving an analysis and for the most part confining his demonstration to the earlier acts. Yet he was not entirely satisfied with his understanding of *Lear,* as is indicated, perhaps, in a letter to Britton in which he wrote, "I have learnt, what I might easily have anticipated, that the Lear of Shakespeare is not a good subject for a whole lecture in my style."[20] He was unable to reconcile himself to the blinding of Gloucester, and he could never satisfactorily explain the characters of Goneril and Regan.[21]

It is one of the characteristics of organic unity that at any time in the process of growth the organism will include all the appearances that have been relevant to it and will contain the potentiality of all that are yet to come. For that reason the first scene of a play is of particular importance. Coleridge makes an explicit statement of the ability of Shakespeare to start a play in accordance with the growth of the action when, listing the methods by which Shakespearean dramas start, he writes, "They . . . place before us in one glance both the past and the future in some effect which implies the continuance and agency of its cause."[22] An understanding of that effect is essential to a correct analysis of the play. In *Othello* Coleridge was particularly anxious to establish the lack of a predisposition towards jealousy in the character of the hero; for Othello is a "high and chivalrous Moorish chief."[23] Unlike the susceptible Macbeth, Othello is basically and entirely honorable: "Iago's suggestions, you see, are quite new to him. They do not correspond with anything of a like nature previously in his mind."[24] In accordance with the nobility and high character of the hero, there is nothing unformed in *Othello*: ". . . everything assumes its due place and proportion, and the whole mature powers of his [Shakespeare's] mind are displayed in admirable equilibrium."[25] Therefore, in the beginning of the play we are introduced to a high character who is marred by a tendency toward suspicion. Our interest in him deepens gradually:

[20] *B.L.,* Vol. II, p. 327.

[21] *Ibid.,* Vol. I, p. 66.

[22] *Ibid.,* p. 41.

[23] *Ibid.,* Vol. II, p. 350.

[24] *Ibid.,* p. 351.

[25] *Ibid.*

"first, our acquaintance,—then friend—then object of anxiety."[26] In his comments on the text, Coleridge stresses the honesty and nobility of the character.[27] It is this fineness of temper in Othello which gives force to the catastrophe and increases enormously the ultimate effect of the play.

Richard II is a purely historical play, and so falls into a different category from the drama proper. Its classification does not depend upon the amount of historical material compared with the fictions, but in the relation of the history to the plot: "In the purely historical plays, the history informs the plot;...in... *Macbeth, Hamlet, Lear* it subserves it."[28] One effect of this is that the work consists of events presented in their results.[29] The spirit of *Richard II,* then, is the spirit of patriotic reminiscence.[30] The very fact that the play is historical, however, serves to make more clear Shakespeare's solution to the problem of interpreting events in such a way as to produce organic unity. Coleridge comments upon Shakespeare's judgment in the introduction of *accidents* which give reality, *individual life*.[31] An illustration of this is the scene between the Queen and the Gardener (Act III, sc. 4), which "realizes the thing, makes the occurrence no longer a segment, but gives an individuality, a liveliness and presence to the scene."[32] Even more striking, however, is Shakespeare's handling of the character of Richard, which forms the center of the play. Here, as in his greatest works, Shakespeare shows in the first scenes "the germ of all the after events, in Richard's insincerity, partiality, arbitrariness, favoritism, and in the proud, tempestuous temperament of his barons."[33] Not only is the character of Richard beautifully conceived, but all the other characters are shown in direct relation to him and form integral parts of the play. Speaking of Gaunt, Coleridge is thoroughly in accord with his philosophy when he writes, "The plays of Shakespeare, as before observed of *Romeo and Juliet,* were characteristic throughout:—whereas *that* was all youth and spring, *this* was womanish weakness; the

[26] *B.L.*, Vol. I, p. 51.   [28] *Ibid.*, p. 143.   [30] *Ibid.*   [32] *Ibid.*, Vol. II, p. 284.
[27] *Ibid.*, pp. 52–53.   [29] *Ibid.*   [31] *Ibid.*, p. 157.   [33] *Ibid.*, Vol. I, p. 153.

characters were of extreme old age, or partook of the nature of age and imbecility."[34] York, also, is illustrative of "the beautiful keeping of the character of the play. He like Gaunt, is old, and, full of a religious loyalty struggling with indignation at the king's vices and follies, is an evidence of a man giving up all energy under a feeling of despair."[35] In this play we see Bolingbroke in contrast to Richard as far as the present is concerned, but we also see in him germs the potentiality of which will be fully realized in *Henry IV.* This linking of historical plays in the way of organic unity is characteristic of Shakespeare, for others besides Bolingbroke can be cited: the preparation in *Henry IV* for the character of Henry V; the character of Gloucester in *Henry VI* which prepares us for Richard III.[36]

Coleridge's treatment of *Richard II* is, on the whole, one of the best examples of the application of his theory to the drama. The use of historical material in a historical way, yet shown as truly organic; the interpretation of the characters as falling, through their relationships, into an integrated whole; the conception of a character in one play which is fully developed in another,—all these things represent the heart of Coleridge's criticism.

Turning now to the criticism of particular speeches, we find equally clear evidence of his theory. His textual comments are often based on his understanding of Shakespeare's style as organic. He criticizes Antony's speech in *Julius Caesar,*

> Pardon me, Julius! Here wast thou bay'd, brave hart;
> Here didst thou fall, and here thy hunters stand,
> Sign'd in thy spoil and crimson'd in thy lethe.
> O world, thou wast the forest to this hart;
> And this, indeed, O world, the heart of thee
> (Act III, sc. 1, ll. 205–209),

doubting the last two lines (as here quoted) because of the change in rhythm; but secondly, and this is more important, "because they interrupt not only the sense and connection, but likewise the flow both of the passion and (what is with me still more de-

[34] *Ibid.,* Vol. II, p. 272   [35] *Ibid.,* p. 280.   [36] *Ibid.,* p. 281.

cisive) the Shakespearean link of association."[37] In other words,
the style is organic in its progressive building of relationships the
integration of which is so apparent that any deviation from it
becomes noticeable. Any true line in Shakespeare will have its
certain place in the pattern of his thought; it will at once be the
result of what has gone before, and the foreshadowing of what
is to come. So it is even with conceits: "Conceits he has, but they
not [only] rise out of some word in the lines before, but they lead
to the thought in the lines following."[38]

Coleridge bases his criticism of the King's speech in *All's Well
That Ends Well* on the same principle.

KING.   Let higher Italy
         Those bated that inherit but the fall
         Of the last monarchy,—see that you come
         Not to woo honor, but to wed it.
                                (Act II, sc. 1, ll. 12–15)

Very apologetically he suggests "bastards" for "bated," on the
grounds, first, that it makes sense out of a passage which is meaningless, and secondly, that the result is peculiarly Shakespearean:
"The following 'wed' and 'woo' are so far confirmative as they
mark Shakespeare's manner of connection by unmarked influences of association from some preceding metaphor. This it is
which makes his style so peculiarly vital and organic."[39] Again we
have a philosophical theory, through a way of regarding relationships, applied definitely to a text.

A slightly different application of the principle is shown in his
comment on Caesar's speech in *Antony and Cleopatra:*

CAESAR.   Most noble Antony,
         Let not the piece of virtue which is set
         Betwixt us as the cement of our love,
         To keep it builded, be the ram to batter
         The fortress of it; for better might we
         Have lov'd without this mean, if on both parts
         This be not cherish'd.
                                (Act III, sc. 2, ll. 27–33)

[37] *B.L.*, Vol. I, p. 17.   [38] *Ibid.*   [39] *Ibid.*, p. 112.

The figure is incongruous, lacking in unity, because it is "an unrepresentable eye-image—a *piece* of—*set* betwixt—as *cement*—turned to a *battering-ram*."[40] The incongruity in the figure is the result of a false relationship. Coleridge's suspicion that the text is corrupt here is based purely upon his assumption of the perfection of Shakespeare's art.

He rarely finds a passage which he is forced to admit is genuine but uncharacteristic of Shakespeare. Such a one was the blinding of Gloucester. Another is the speech of Oliver in *As You Like It* where Oliver plans the death of Orlando and at the same time enumerates Orlando's good qualities. Coleridge feels in this speech an incongruity between the expressed truths and the malignant feelings of Oliver.[41] A union of these two things is forced and artificial; it is contrary to the truth of nature and therefore lacks unity. However, in keeping with his humility before Shakespeare, Coleridge declares that it is "too venturous" to make such an accusation, and will not be greatly surprised if hereafter it appears to him as a fresh beauty.[42]

Though Coleridge is humble before Shakespeare, he is not when confronted with other writers. In fact, Shakespeare is repeatedly used as the criterion by which others are judged. So it is with Ben Jonson. His *Epicoene* is farce rather than comedy, because comedy demands characters whereas a farce needs only caricatures. According to Coleridge, the defect in Morose is "that the accident is not a prominence growing out of, and nourished by, the character which still circulates in it, but that the character, such as it is, rises out of, or rather consists in, the accident."[43] The features of Shakespeare's comic characters, on the other hand, are "exquisitely characteristic," irrespective of how disproportionate and laughable they may be.[44] The distinction is the familiar one with Coleridge, that Shakespeare conceives characters in terms of organic unity, so that no matter how far they may go from reality, they still represent a consistent and proportionate

---

[40] *Ibid.*, pp. 88–89.   [42] *Ibid.*   [44] *Ibid.*

[41] *Ibid.*, p. 104.   [43] *Works*, 1847 ed., Vol. XIV, p. 280.

growth; whereas with Jonson there is no growth, no proportionately developed center; there is merely an artificial description
which results in a lifeless character: "But Jonson's are either a
man with a huge wen, having a circulation of its own and which
we might conceive amputated, and the patient thereby losing all
his character; or they are mere wens themselves instead of men,—
wens personified, or with eyes, nose, and mouth cut out, man-
drake fashion."[45]

The distinction Coleridge makes between Jonson's and Shakespeare's characters is merely an expression in detail of the distinction between the two men as artists. They are ultimately different
in kind: "Let its [Jonson's kind] inferiority to the Shakespearean
be at once fairly owned,—but at the same time as the inferiority
of an altogether different *genus* of the drama."[46] In another place,
Coleridge states that difference concretely: "The one [Shake-
speare] was to present a model by imitation of real life, taking
from real life all that in it which it ought to be, and supplying the
rest;—the other is a copy of what is, and as it is,—at best a toler-
able, but most frequently a blundering copy."[47] His use of the
word "imitation" is significant here, implying as it does the process of conceiving life organically, as opposed to the word "copy,"
which implies a mechanical conception. In short, Coleridge's
criticism of Jonson is that Jonson could achieve only a mechanical
superimposition of plot on material, enlivened by an accurate and
minute account of realistic detail.

I have already spoken of Coleridge's criticism of Beaumont and
Fletcher and his comparison of them to Shakespeare. They are
judged by the usual structural standard and found wanting except in comparatively short passages. Indeed, so sure is Coleridge
of his ground here that he flares up at the suggestion that Shakespeare is inferior in so much as a single line. Seward preferred
Alphonso's poisoning in *A Wife for a Month* to the passage in *King
John*, Act V, sc. 7. Coleridge's comment is characteristic: "Mr.
Seward! Mr. Seward! you may be, and I trust you are, an angel;

---

[45] *Works*, 1847 ed., Vol. XIV, p. 280.   [46] *Ibid*.   [47] *Ibid*.

but you were an ass."[48] His criticism of *Rollo* illustrates his general opinion. The play is "perhaps the most energetic of Fletcher's tragedies" but "he was not philosopher enough to bottom his original." That is, Fletcher could not conceive a character organically; he could merely attribute actions to fictitious personages. So in *Rollo*, in which "he evidently aimed at a new Richard III . . . he has produced a mere personification of outrageous wickedness, with no fundamental characteristic impulses to make either the tyrant's words or actions intelligible."[49] Philosophically, "intelligible" means, of course, that the character does not reveal, and is not in accordance with the pattern of, nature. Again, the very progression of the scenes shows Fletcher's failure to grasp the true principle of unity. The best scene in the play (Baldwin's sentence in the third act) renders the afterscene "not only unnatural, but disgusting." Obviously, each succeeding scene should catch up the strands of the play and, in becoming a part of the whole, add to the cumulative effect.

---

[48] *Ibid.*, p. 291.

[49] *Ibid.*, p. 313.

IX. CONCLUSION

Arthur symons once wrote, "*The Biographia Literaria* is the greatest book of criticism in English, and one of the most annoying books in any language."[1] The judgment is applicable to the entire body of Coleridge's critical writings. However, the annoyance of any reader may have two sources. The more obvious one is the lack of orderly plan and development—a lack characteristic of all Coleridge's work. It is regrettable, but nothing can be done about it. Professor Raysor's recent edition of the criticism is the ultimate in clear presentation, yet the very accuracy of his scholarship serves to emphasize the disorderliness of the material with which he deals. That is the Coleridge, diffuse, repetitious, digressive, whom we must accept. His was an intensely active mind which lacked the will to act. It was not without reason that he once remarked, "I have a smack of Hamlet myself, if I may say so."[2] I should say that he had considerably more than a smack. There is good reason to believe that the audiences at his lectures felt the same way. Crabbe Robinson, in a letter to Mrs. Clarkson, tells of an incident which occurred at one of the lectures. Coleridge had concluded his remarks upon Hamlet with the assertion that action is the great end of all; that no intellect, however grand, is valuable if it draw us from action and lead us to think and think till the time for action has passed and we can do nothing. Robinson repeats this, and continues, "Somebody said to me, 'This is a satire on himself.' 'No,' said I, 'it is an elegy.' "[3]

The second source of annoyance lies in the failure of many readers to understand what Coleridge is saying, and the feeling that the criticism would be much better without any attempts on the part of Coleridge to deal with philosophy and explain the principles he is using. Such an objection goes to the heart of the matter. If we reduce his criticism to a collection of isolated but brilliant remarks or passages, we ignore what was to Coleridge

---

[1] *Dramatis Personae*, p. 94.   [2] Raysor, *op. cit.*, Vol. II, p. 352.   [3] *Ibid.*, p. 229.

fundamentally valuable, namely, the statement of the principles by which writing is accomplished.

That he succeeded in both stating and applying his principles, I have attempted to demonstrate. The central part of his criticism lies in the idea of organic unity, and he is amazingly consistent in his application of that principle. His mind seems to have been so absorbed with it that it became a natural way of looking at the world rather than a rule mechanically applied.

Yet there is a conflict of principles in his thought, a conflict which he never formally recognized. There is undeniably present on the one hand the idea of reconciliation of opposites, and on the other there is his central principle of organic unity. It did not occur to him, apparently, that these two were in conflict, and that although both were idealistic, formed from the same stuff, they represented different systems of thought. He makes use of them interchangeably as suits his convenience. But the greater richness of concrete application, the larger view, and the greater flexibility of organic unity give that theory a predominant position in his thought. His foreshadowing of Bosanquet's aesthetics is clearly evident; the detailed correspondence between the two men is amazing. He seems to be possessed of all the essential apparatus of Bosanquet, and he has in addition an incomparably finer emotional understanding of literature.

No critic repays close scrutiny more richly than Coleridge. His particular insights are valuable in themselves and have been praised enough elsewhere. But, much more important, he offers a system and a technique of criticism. His system has the advantage of being at the same time specific and flexible. The specific quality must be insisted upon. It is obvious that any idealistic critic will be interested more in the structure of his material than its immediate beauties; that the productions of such different critics as Arnold and Pater will not exemplify the idealistic technique. A significant comparison centering around the part played by system in criticism could be made between Coleridge and Dryden. Dryden's criticism embodies a struggle between, on the one hand, a system which had long outlived its usefulness and become antiquated, and, on the other, a fresh, original sensitiveness to literature. Neoclassicism could not accommodate and give form to the insights which Dryden achieved. With Coleridge, the system was taking form as he used it. It became a completely held world view which was particularly applicable to literature. With Coleridge there is a constant interaction between the special insights and the system. The insights illuminate and enrich the system, and the system, because it is a general way of looking at the world, tends to produce more insights.

The union of insights and system was hardly a matter of chance. Both by background and by temperament Coleridge was eminently suited to be his sort of critic. He could no more avoid either his speculative or his emotional side than Shakespeare could avoid writing organically. The emphasis placed upon system should not be misleading. No scheme can ever work as a touchstone for literature. One of the virtues of Coleridge's principle is that it cannot be used as a rule of thumb, that in the hands of an unfeeling person it becomes meaningless. It was not so with Coleridge. The combination of a poet's heart and a philosopher's head served to produce a criticism which ranks with the finest that has been written.

LIST OF BOOKS CITED

BOSANQUET, *Principle of Individuality and Value*, London, 1912.

BOSANQUET, *Three Lectures on Aesthetic*, London, 1915.

CAMPAGNAC, *The Cambridge Platonists*, Oxford, 1901.

COLERIDGE, *Anima Poetae*, London, 1895.

COLERIDGE, *Biographia Literaria*, Oxford, 1907.

COLERIDGE, *The Friend*, New York, 1884.

COLERIDGE, *Letters*, 1895.

COLERIDGE, *Miscellanies, Aesthetic and Literary*, London, 1895.

COLERIDGE, *Poetical Works*, London, 1924.

COLERIDGE, *Shakespearean Criticism*, Cambridge, 1930.

COLERIDGE, *Works*, London, 1847.

HÖFFDING, *History of Modern Philosophy*, London, 1924.

HOWARD, *Coleridge's Idealism*, Boston, 1924.

LAMB, *Works*, New York, 1903.

LITCHFIELD, *Tom Wedgewood*, London, 1903.

MARET, *Anthropology*, London, 1912.

MUIRHEAD, *Coleridge as a Philosopher*, London, 1930.

PERRY, *Present Philosophical Tendencies*, London, 1929.

POWELL, *A Romantic Theory of Poetry*, London, 1926.

RAYSOR, *Coleridge's Shakespearean Criticism*, Cambridge, 1930.

RICHARDS, *Coleridge on Imagination*, London, 1934.

SAINTSBURY, *History of Criticism*, Edinburgh, 1900.

SCHELLING, *Werke*, Stuttgart, 1858.

SNYDER, *Critical Principle of the Reconciliation of Opposites*, Ann Arbor, 1918.

SYMONS, *Dramatis Personae*, Indianapolis, 1923.

TULLOCH, *Rational Theology in England*, London, 1874.

DATE DUE